Patternmaking in practice

a step by step guide

Patternmaking
in practice
a step by step guide   Lucia Mors de Castro

Original project: **maomao** publications

Editorial coordination: Anja Llorella Oriol
Author: Lucia Mors de Castro
Texts: Lucia Mors de Castro
Photographies: Magdalena Lepka
Model: Anke Schmiedeberg
English translation: Cillero & de Motta
Copyediting: Cillero & de Motta
Art direction and layout: Emma Termes Parera

PROMOPRESS is a brand of:
PROMOTORA DE PRENSA INTERNACIONAL, S. A.
Ausiàs March, 124
08013 Barcelona, Spain
Tel.: +34 93 245 14 64
Fax: +34 93 265 48 83
E-mail: info@promopress.es
www.promopress.info

First published in English: 2010
ISBN: 978-84-92810-07-9
Printed in Spain

Get down off the rack and be creative

When we look at the history of fashion, we realize the significance of the "cut", which marks the beginning of pattern making in the history of clothing development. From simply wrapping up in a piece of cloth, which was used to cover part or all of the body, the method of tailoring and sewing the fabric has gradually developed to make the garment fit the shape of the body. In many non-Western cultures basic rectangular shapes (whose width is generally determined by the width of the loom) are still very much the norm. Nevertheless, a customized fit is only achieved by wrapping the fabric around the body. Wraps have many practical advantages. They provide protection against heat and cold and can thus easily be made to suit individual needs. Through the use of belts and clasps it is possible to make an infinite number of different styles, with tiny objects being carried in the folds. Even babies can be transported in a simple, convenient manner. The bolts of cloth themselves are easy to store and transport, either folded or in rolls, which is particularly important in nomadic cultures. They fulfill a great many functions and last but by no means least, one size fits all.

However, in the culture of Western Europe, fashion dictates otherwise. Back in the Middle Ages, garments that were cut and sewn soon replaced the large rectangles and semicircles. Cleverly cut and stitched materials supplant the simple geometric shapes, fitting snug against the body or reshaping it, offering the wearer the task or opportunity of selecting something new to wear each day.

Cutting out soon leads to tailoring or dressmaking. With curved cuts, shaped seams, and the insertion of darts and godets, it is possible to create artistic, three-dimensional garments from the fabric. Contemporary fashion designers are using the experience gleaned from the past 800 years to experiment and are constantly coming up with ever newer and more amazing ideas, by playing around with different combinations of mathematical pattern construction, draping and tailoring.

This book gives an insight into the processes that contributes towards the creation of custom-made clothing. First we start with the sketch and the fabric samples, before moving on to taking measurements, shaping the material to the pattern, then tailoring and stitching, and last of all, the finished garment. The book focuses on introducing the reader to the technique of creating dressmaking patterns by hand, along with all the intermediate stages that teach us how to transfer the pattern to paper, from the mere idea to its artistic representation on cloth. It is particularly designed with motivated beginners in mind, who want to make their own tailor-made clothing and see their boundless imagination recreated in fabric. With a little perseverance, the reader will learn to understand and follow the procedure by firstly transferring the two-dimensional basic design to paper and subsequently to the three-dimensional shape of the body. Once on paper, this design will provide the fundamental basis for all future shapes and pattern alterations.

The reader is led right from the opening pages of the book into the craft of working with paper and fabric. A graphic overview is presented of the materials and tools required, along with the instructions for taking and calculating the measurements needed for the technical aspects of pattern making.

The chapter devoted to shaping darts explains the basic technique of drafting the model lines and shows how the basic pattern can be altered without compromising the perfect fit.

The explanation provided for constructing the basic cut on a mannequin gives an idea of how to go about "tackling" the three-dimensional body. The exercise of working directly with curves, inserting darts and taking in flat seams should lead to a deeper understanding of how the actual shape of the basic pattern is arrived at.

The criteria for choosing the cloth, how it is cut and tailored, the procedure for the seam allowances, explanations for tracing the lining, performing a correct fitting, along with various hand and machine stitches, are all helpful learning tips that will enable the reader to create their own design.

Step-by-step instructions offer very clear explanations about how to tailor the cut for the skirt, top and sleeves, and how to move on to develop techniques to use these basic cuts to create our own designs. Brief explanations are also provided offering details of the sewing process, such as the steps to follow to insert a dart, sew in a zipper, or how to add a facing to a top. The final chapter also provides a basic knowledge of collar design and offers further useful tips concerning the virtually unlimited number of variations available for basic patterns.

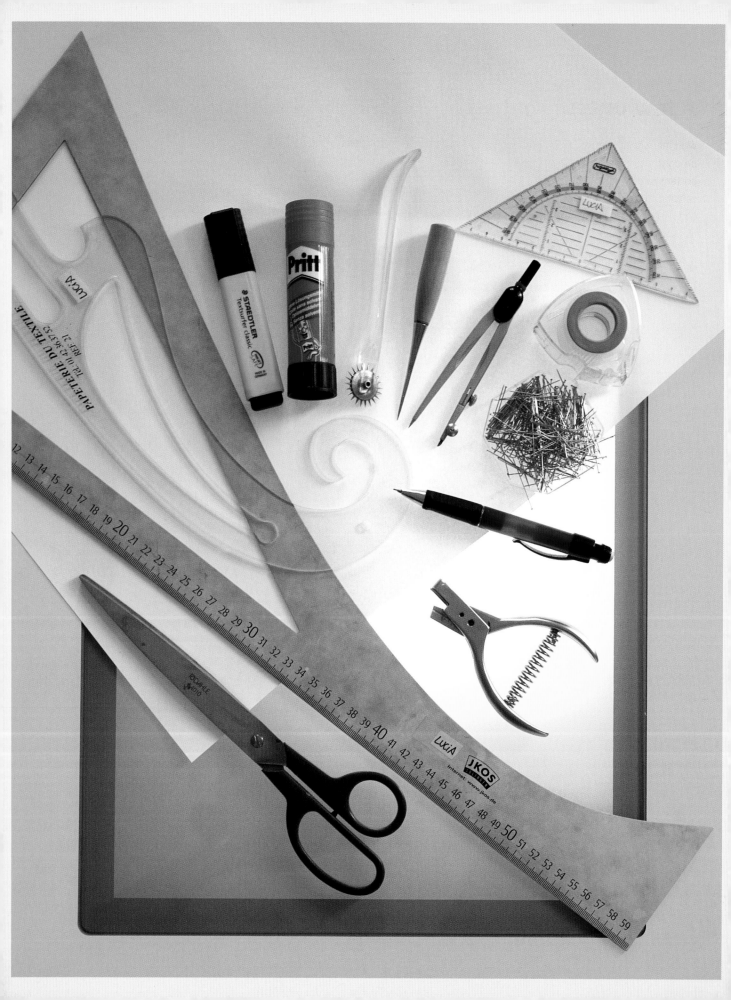

A few useful materials and tools

Working with paper and fabric is only productive when it can be done easily by hand. So materials and tools have a very important part to play, and thus it is worth investing in them. The selection discussed below only cover the basic equipment and can be extended virtually ad infinitum. However, it is up to each designer to find out the method and means that give the best results for their specific patterns.

For sketching the pattern

Initially, packing paper is probably sufficient if large quantities are not required. However, for more complex work, it is worth investing in large rolls of paper such as those used for plotters. The paper should be tear-resistant and easy to cut. Some pattern designers prefer to use paper that is almost transparent because it is better for tracing the lines.

A propelling pencil is recommended for drawing and a color marker for labeling. For the accurate construction of a pattern, it is important to have rulers and tailor's squares, particularly a large T-square with a 60-centimeter-long blade, which will greatly facilitate large-scale work.

The procedure for using French curves with various contours needs a certain amount of practice. The rulers should be placed on the paper in such a way that the required curve can be drawn. Sometimes it is necessary to interrupt the drawing of a line to move the ruler to a new position. To draw two identical curves, we recommend making small markings on the ruler or else tracing the line in question.

Weights are needed to hold the paper down. To assemble the parts it is best to use pins without plastic heads, since these allow the paper and fabric to lie flat. Using a magnetic or wrist pin cushion means that they are always close at hand.

Likewise, another handy feature is removable adhesive tape or masking tape, which can be used to stick points together temporarily and then unstick them again without doing any damage. For permanent joins, instead of tape, it is better to use a pritt stick since this means the pattern can still be ironed.

Sharp paper scissors can be used to cut the pattern out accurately while protecting hands and joins. For the cross markings lines, i.e. the markings at the edges of the pattern, there is a tool that works like a small notcher. The ends can of course also be trimmed with scissors. When shifting points a small tool with a metal tip is required. This makes a tiny hole in the paper. When shifting lines, these are traced or perforated with a small tracing wheel. A pocket calculator and a pair of compasses might be helpful.

During the modeling process we recommend making several exact copies of the pattern. Quasi-transparent paper or a sheet of glass lit from below will facilitate the process, since it is often necessary to make cuts or stick additions, and once cut, it is usually very difficult to return to a previous stage, whether to make an adjustment or when the pattern is to serve as the basis for a new garment.

For measuring purposes:

To measure a person, a waist binding can be helpful. This is a measuring tape with a little hook on one end and approximately 60 holes on the other to enable it to be closed. It is placed on the natural waist line and used as a reference point for other measurements. Using another flexible measuring tape, it is possible to take the other measurements. A strip of paper can be used to help measure the back height. To avoid cutting below the arm we recommend folding the paper twice and place it under the arm with the fold face upwards. Detailed instructions on how to take measurements are given on page 12.

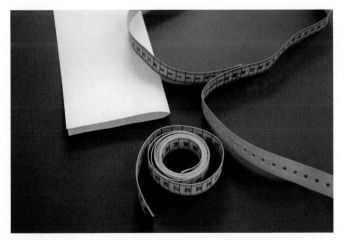

Marking the fabric

In order to transfer the cut plus seam allowances to the fabric in an orderly way, use a tailor's square or ruler and mark the material on the wrong side of the fabric with tailor's chalk or a pencil. For markings on the right side of the fabric, there are chalks that can be erased by ironing.

For cutting out the fabric

Once the seam allowances have been marked, we can proceed to cut out the fabric. To do this we need some long sharp scissors for cutting out fabric, which must be comfortable to hold. For making notches on the edge of the fabric small scissors or a pincer are used. Markings on the cloth such as darts, or the position of pockets or buttons are made with pins or thread on all layers of the fabric.

Sewing accessories

A large range of helpful and essential tools and notions exist for preparing the fabric. Among others, these include interfacing, which can be ironed into place, seam binding, buttons, zippers and elastic. Finding out about all the resources available before you start sewing, and investing in them, is usually rewarded by a more successful outcome.

Ironing

One essential stage in the sewing process is ironing. Even this can be simplified considerably by using certain utensils. The basic equipment consists of a good steam iron with a Teflon soleplate and a clean, firmly padded ironing board. A sleeve ironing board makes it easier to press the seams on narrow items of clothing. A water spray and an ironing cloth are other items that are useful for fixing interfacing in place. Cardboard templates can help when ironing fabric edges. A tape measure should always be kept handy to ensure the work is accurate.

Taking measurements

During the early stages of tailoring the individual pattern, detailed measurements are taken of the body. The pattern designer should pay close attention to the body that is to wear the garment, looking at it from all angles and noting the proportions and any individual peculiarities. In addition to the measurements taken using professional methods, sketches of the person's silhouette are often used as helpful reminders to capture the contours or the distribution of the measurements on the three-dimensional body. Two people will always be needed to take measurements, since the person being measured should adopt a natural stance in an upright position. The measurements are taken with the tape measure flush against the body or on a thin layer of cloth.

First of all a waist binding should be placed around the body. This is a measuring tape with a little hook on one end and approximately 60 holes on the other so that it can be closed. The hook can thus be hooked up at the right spot to obtain the waist circumference (WAC). The waist binding should remain at the narrowest part of the torso (the natural waist line) while the measurements are being taken, since this line is often taken as a reference point for calculating other body measurements.

Next we measure the bust circumference (BC). To do this, the tape measure is placed over the highest part of the bust at the front, and then passed around the body underneath the arms, raising it slightly in the area of the shoulder blades at the back.

The hip circumference (HC) is the horizontal circumference of the body measured in the area of the most pronounced part of the bottom and the broadest part of the pelvis. The position of the tape measure should be carefully checked in all places, since both the bottom and the thighs and lateral contours of the hips are crucial for determining the size.

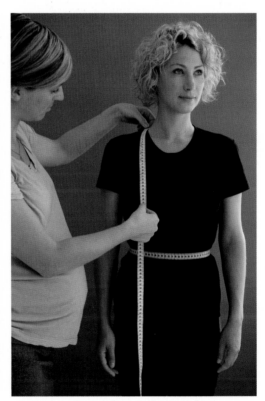

The distance between the hip circumference (HC) and the waistline gives us the individual hip depth (HD), which is usually about 19 — 22 cm measured from the waist down.

The tape measure is then placed on the front down from the first vertebra. The bust depth (BD) is measured directly on the tip of the bust.

The front length (FL) goes from the base of the neck to the lower edge of the waistline.

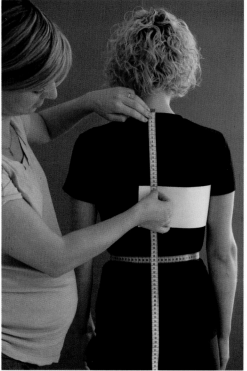

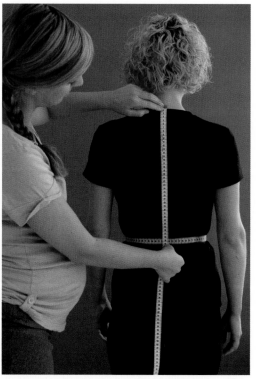

The measurement of the back height (BAH) fixes the position and depth of the armhole. To calculate this value, we use a strip of paper as an aid, placing it right under the arm and extending it to the spine. The first vertebra should be noted as a reference point for the tape measure. The back height is obtained at the top edge of the horizontal strip of paper.

The back length (BL) is also measured from the upper point on the base of the neck to the lower edge of the waistline. The back length is, like the front length, one of the most important measurements involving position, which means we can extract information about the possibility of a stooped posture from such data. This value should be measured very precisely and its difference checked against the measurement chart.

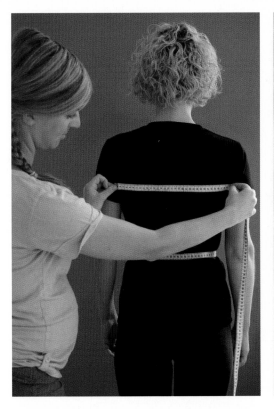 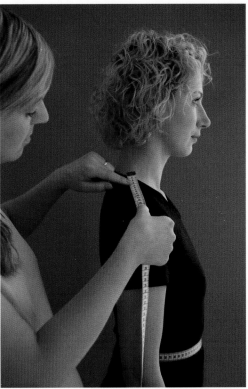

The back width (BAW) is calculated approximately at the height of the bust circumference over the lower part of the shoulder blades. It should be measured flat across the back from one sleeve insertion point to the other, at the place where two sharp folds are formed when the person's arms are hanging loose by their side, which marks the intersection between the back and the arms.

With the following measurement we calculate the shoulder width (SW). For the shoulder width we take the tape measure from the edge of the neck opening to the shoulder bone.

The position of the elbow is calculated by extending the tape measure to its outer tip.

Prolonging this line to the outer wrist will give us the sleeve length (SL).
This measurement passes over the outer point of the slightly bent elbow, since the sleeve length should be the longest distance.

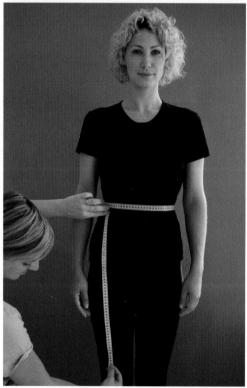

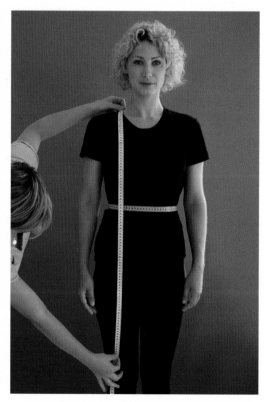

The skirt or dress length is normally determined in accordance with the relevant design and can therefore not be considered to be a set value. Nevertheless, it is worth fixing the height of the knee and/or ankle to have a subsequent reference for the length of the garment.

Measuring chart

The measurements obtained are compared against the values in the measuring chart (page 18) and assigned a dress-making size. To do this, we shall use the bust circumference (BC) as a reference, selecting the dress-making size that is closest to our bust circumference.

In so doing it is sometimes observed that the other measurement results do not coincide with those on the list, and that some measurements are missing. At this point the following data should be indicated: the main measurements for the body height (BH), bust circumference (BC), waist circumference (WAC), hip circumference (HC), distance between the widest part of the hip to the waist line (individual hip depth, HD) and sleeve length (SL) should always be measured snug against the body and used specifically for the pattern.

The additional measurements, such as the back height (BAH), back length (BL), hip depth (HD), bust depth (BD), front length (FL), and back width (BAW) are measured and then checked against the measuring chart. In case of doubt, as a beginner, it is better to use the measurements calculated.

The neck (N), armhole diameter (AD) and bust width (BW) are always calculated. This is so because such measurements are difficult to get and the risk of making a mistake is very high. With the aid of the following formulas, it is possible to calculate these measurements (from a BC of 80 cm).

N neck	*1/10 of 1/2 BC + 2 cm*
AD armhole diameter	*1/8 BC % 1.5 cm*
BW bust width	*1/4 BC % 4 cm*

In order to obtain a certain amount of free movement in the garment, the allowances for the back height (BAH), back width (BAW), armhole diameter (AD) and bust width (BW), along with the bust circumference (BC) should be taken into account.

The allowance will depend on the model in question, the material used and the clothing tastes of each individual; however, the following allowances can be used for guidance:

	Dress	Fitted jacket	Loose-fitting jacket	Trenchcoat or overcoat
BAH	1 cm	1.5 - 2 cm	2 – 2.5 cm	3 – 3.5 cm
BAW	0.5 cm	1 cm	1 - 1.5 cm	1.5 - 2 cm
AD	1.5 cm	2 cm	2.5 - 3 cm	3 - 4 cm
BW	1.5 cm	1.5 - 2 cm	2 cm	2 – 2.5 cm
1/2 BC	3.5 cm	4.5 - 5 cm	5.5 – 6.5 cm	6.5–8.5 cm

Sheet of measurements

The sheet of measurements illustrated, which can be used as a template, serves to gather together all the measurements required to create the first pattern. In this way we can proceed with the confidence of knowing that we have not forgotten any measurements and that they have all been calculated without any errors.

It is possible to represent the contours of the body directly on the sketch of the basic pattern and the mannequin. The observations for the mannequin are better carried out at a certain distance. An exact observation at this point will facilitate many decisions that need to be taken later on.

It is especially important to identify any anomalies, or deviations from the "normal body", even though this "normal body" does not really exist. A bent, crooked or very rigid posture, uneven shoulder height, large shoulder blades, the height and shape of the bust, the shape of the belly and hips, a hollow back, large thighs, calves, and knees are some of the main features that need to be taken into account. While the pattern is being constructed and also during the fitting stage, these specific characteristics should be checked and adjusted time and time again.

The basic measurements taken are noted at the top of the sheet of measurements, that is to say, the normal sizes as stated on the measuring chart set out on page 18: body height (BH), bust circumference (BC), waist circumference (WAC), hip circumference (HC) and the individual hip depth (HD), i.e. the vertical distance measured from the hip line to the waist line, and the shoulder width (SW). The halves, quarters, and eighths of the measurements speed up the process in the subsequent creation of the pattern design.

The following values should be referred to when consulting the measuring chart or when calculated using the formulas. Furthermore, the data is also entered in accordance with the model and material, added together and calculated to obtain the final sum.

The sleeve length (SL), upper arm circumference (UAC) and the required sleeve hem width (SHW) are measured and recorded. The sleeve head height (SHH) and the sleeve width (SLW) are calculated according to the appropriate formulas.

Once the sheet of measurements has been fully completed, we are ready to begin with the specific task of constructing the basic patterns.

	Measurement	Measurements in cm						
S	Size	6/8	8/10	10/12	12/14	14/16	16/18	18/20
BH	Body height	168	168	168	168	168	168	168
BC	Bust circumference	80	84	88	92	96	100	104
WAC	Waist circumference	64	68	72	76	80	84	88
HC	Hip circumference	91	94	97	100	103	106	109
BNC	Base of the neck circumference	34,8	35,4	36	36,6	37,2	37,8	38,4
N	Neck	6,5	6,6	6,7	6,8	6,9	7	7,1
BAH	Back height	19,3	19,7	20,1	20,5	20,9	21,3	21,7
BL	Back length	41,2	41,4	41,6	41,8	42	42,2	42,4
HD	Hip depth	61,4	61,8	62,2	62,6	63	63,4	63,8
BD	Bust depth	26,5	27,3	28,1	28,9	29,7	30,5	31,3
FL	Front length	44,1	44,7	45,3	45,9	46,5	47,1	47,7
BAW	Back width	15,5	16	16,5	17	17,5	18	18,5
AD	Armhole diameter	7,9	8,6	9,3	10	10,7	11,4	12,1
BW	Bust width	16,6	17,4	18,2	19	19,8	20,6	21,4
SW	Shoulder width	11,8	12	12,2	12,4	12,6	12,8	13
SL	Sleeve length	59,3	59,6	59,9	60,2	60,5	60,8	61,1
UAC	Upper arm circumference	25,6	26,8	28	29,2	30,4	31,6	32,8
WC	Wrist circumference	15	15,4	15,8	16,2	16,6	17	17,4
ABC	Angle of bust dart	11,5°	13°	14,5°	16°	17,5°	19°	20,5°

Sheet of measurements				
Name:		Worked for:	Date:	
Observations on the figure:				
Posture:				

Standard size	Measured	1/2	1/4	1/8
BH (Body height)				
BC (Bust circumference)				
WAC (Waist circumference)				
HC (Hip circumference)				
Individual hip depth (identifies the interval at the greatest point HC to WAC)				

Standard values	Measured	Balanced out	Allowance	Position
1/2 BNC (Base of the neck circumference)				
N (Neck)				
BAH (Back height)				
BL (Back length)				
HD (Hip depth)				
BD (Bust depth)				
FL (Front length)				
BAW (Back width)				
AD (Armhole diameter)				
BW (Bust width)				
1/2 BC (Bust circumference)				

Sleeve measurements	Measured	Formula/Allowance		Positioning
SW (Shoulder width)				
SL (Sleeve length)				
SHH (Sleeve head height)		BAH % 5 to 6 cm		
SLW (Sleeve width)		AD + allowance + 4.5 to 5.5 cm		
UAC (Upper arm circumference)		+ allowance 3 to 5 cm		
EC (Elbow circumference)				
WC (Wrist circumference)				
SHW (Sleeve hem width)				

Darts – A shaping element in pattern making

Darts are triangular or diamond-shaped, tapering, sewn tucks, which are used to add shape and fit the cloth to the contours of the body. In order for the flat cloth to fit the figure on the shoulders, bust, waist and hipline, the darts need to be sewn or else set in the seams, which can in turn be used to add shape to the garment. Darts therefore have fixed places in basic dressmaking. However, they do not always coincide with the idea created in the pattern design. For this reason darts have an important role to play during the designing process. The aim is to maintain the effect of shaping darts, while subordinating their placement and distribution with respect to the seam lines as required by the design. This is done either by placing them as inconspicuously as possible, hidden underneath pockets, for example, or else by using them quite deliberately as decorative elements.

The markings on the model lines should never be drawn on top of the darts. It is better to shift the darts slightly to one side, if they are in the way and, where necessary, move them to an appropriate position inside the seam.

The following exercises illustrate the options available for the pattern maker when inserting darts in a waist length top. When transferring the design, the pattern is clipped at the place where the dart will be inserted. In theory they can be placed in any direction, it only being necessary to ensure that the tip of the dart always remains in its original position. The original dart can be shifted later on to make the width cover the required area.

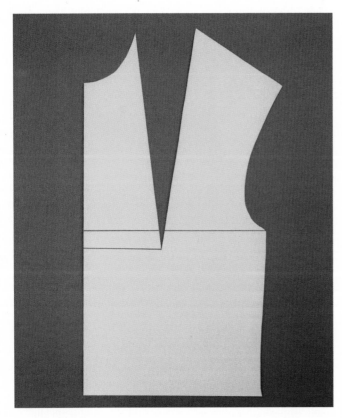

In the basic design the bust dart descends vertically from the point where the shoulder meets the neckline to the most prominent part of the bust, known as the bust apex. During the fitting stage of the basic cut, corrections can be made to improve their placement.

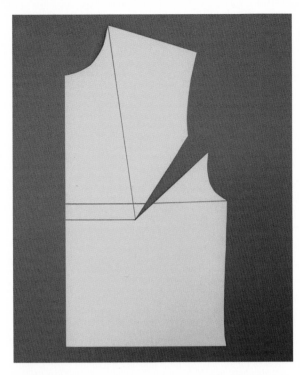

In this case, the dart is inserted in the armhole. This dart will be shorter, while still having the same effect. In this position the dart not only serves a purpose but is also less conspicuous, since it is almost totally concealed by the sleeve.

Here, in its oblique position on the waistline, the dart can fulfill its shaping function and adds an attractive, unusual detail to the garment. The oblique position accentuates the slim feminine waistline.

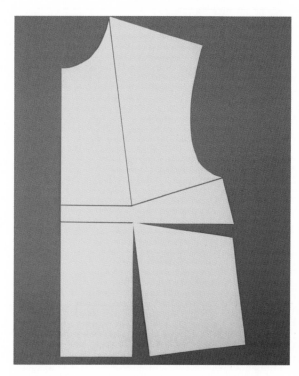

Instead of removing the full width of the dart at just one point, its fullness can also be distributed between two different places, designing two moderately broad darts to make the front panel of the garment a bit softer.

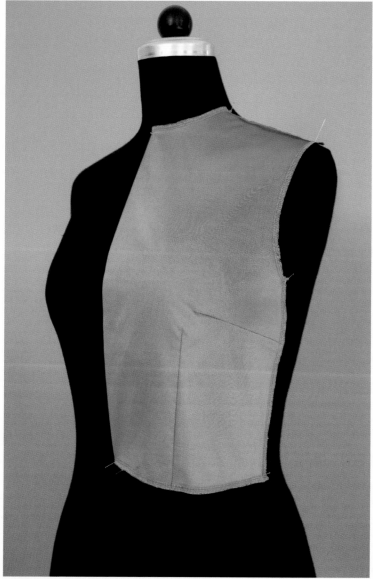

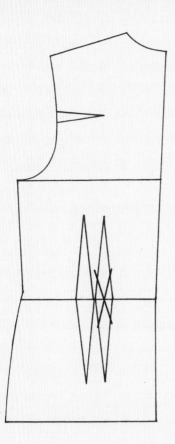

A dart can be shifted even a minimal amount to a parallel position, if required by the design. It should be noted, however, that it will coincide more closely with the contours of the body in its original position. Therefore a dart should only be shifted from its original placement as far as is absolutely necessary to another parallel position, in keeping with the requirements of the design. It is recommended that this movement be limited to about 3 – 4 cm.

The procedure for inserting a dart can also be used to remove it as such. Its volume –like its relocation– however is not lost, but merely "runs" in a different direction. Unlike relocation, however, it is not stitched into this new position but used for extra fullness or else to gain extra width at the skirt hem, as can be seen in the example.

Darts that are left over, as a result of dropping the waistline on a skirt, for example, with very little depth, can be removed if the small amount of extra width can be taken up at the nearest seam (such as the side seam, for example).

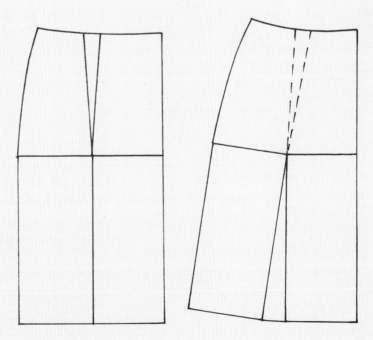

Modeling – The real design begins with the basic cut

The most direct form of creative tailoring is modeling. This is where we work directly with the fabric on the mannequin or person's body, developing a certain shape or an entire garment to produce something that is unique. The pattern can, however, also be obtained from the model by transferring the exact tracings and markings to paper once the piece has been cut. Likewise, it is also possible to reproduce the design after the modeling process.

Modeling is the direct, physical search for form and, as such, often involves trial and error, following up ideas and seeking results to arrive at the perfect fit and completely new designs and creations. Modeling is crucial for understanding the tailoring involved in the process, with the following simple exercises clearly illustrating the procedure for developing the pattern for the top and skirt. The work is carried out on a mannequin using pins and a generously cut non-elastic piece of fabric sample, or muslin toile.

When the cloth is laid out, the straight grain of the fabric should be arranged perpendicularly. In this respect the selvage should be used as a reference. One part of the basic pattern reproduces the left half of the corresponding part of the dress, i.e. one quarter of the body circumference. The resulting paper pattern should therefore be either cut out twice as a mirror image or else placed on the fold of the fabric.

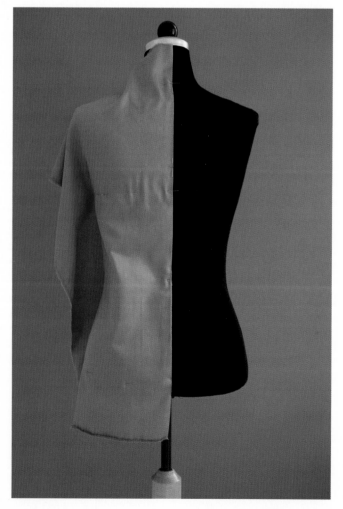

Developing the top
We should begin by placing the fabric vertically on the back of the mannequin. The upper edge should extend at least 3 cm above the base of the neck, but can be cut to make it easier to tuck and fold.

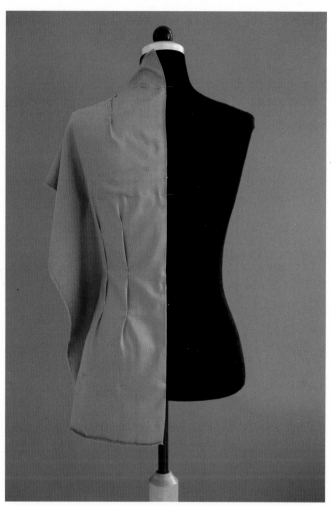

The fabric is smoothed out at the back and pinned on the side seam from the armhole down to the hips. Crosswise tacking stitches should run along the shoulder blade. The excess width at the waist is taken up in two darts, which are evenly distributed between the center back and the side seam. Logically, the deepest part of the dart is located at the narrowest point of the mannequin, which is the waist circumference, and runs up to the bust line and down towards the hips.

Next the fabric at the neckline and outer shoulder edge should be defined. It can soon be seen that a dart is required to shape the shoulder. This should lie roughly in the middle of the shoulder at a right angle and taper out gradually towards the shoulder blade.

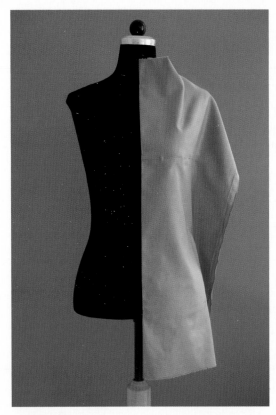

With the front piece, we start in the middle of the mannequin again, making sure that the crosswise threads are horizontal at the height of the bust. The fabric is pinned above the bust and from the underarm down to the hips.

The excess width between the center front and the side seam is taken up in a dart at the waist. This dart should be positioned roughly in the middle and taper out at the bust point, so that the upper part of the garment fits properly.

Then the fabric between the shoulder and armhole is smoothed out and the excess width is taken up in a dart, which rises from the neckline. The top dart also extends to the bust point.

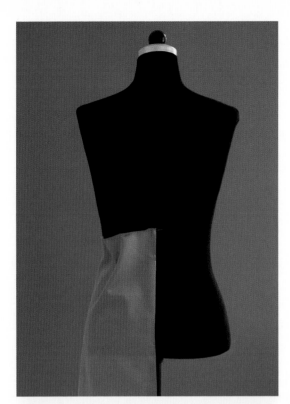

Developing the skirt

The rectangular piece of fabric is placed on the vertical center line down the back. The lengthwise threads run vertically, and therefore the crosswise threads should run horizontally on the hips.

Then the outer point of the hip is pinned and the fabric is smoothed out over the waist. The excess width is taken up at the waist in one or two darts with a length of approximately 13 – 15 cm.

The front panel is treated in a similar way except that here the dart slants almost parallel to the side seam. The intake, or difference between the waistline and the hips (which therefore needs to be taken in), is normally smaller at the front than at the back, because the abdomen usually has a smaller curvature than the bottom. Consequently, the intake at the front can be taken up in a single dart.

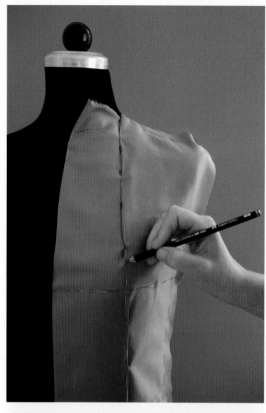

Once the garment has been fitted, the outer edges, darts, seams and cuts should be marked with a pen or tailor's chalk before being removed from the mannequin.

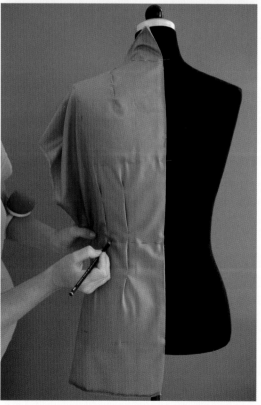

Care must be taken to ensure that the front and back meet perfectly at the side and shoulder seams. Markings on the waist, bust and hip line, along with the sleeves and neckline, make it easier to create an accurate basic paper pattern.

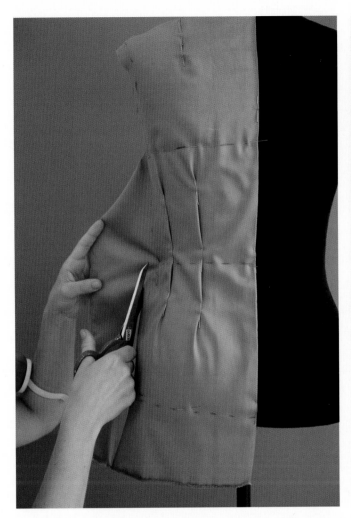 

Excess fabric is trimmed so that it does not "get in the way", in other words, so that it does not hamper the shape of the garment. The top in the basic pattern should reach the hip line. The skirt starts at the waist and has a length of about 60 cm.

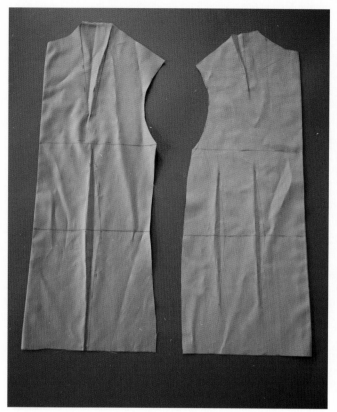 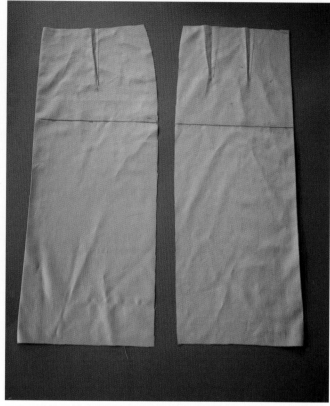

All the pins can now be removed, the seam allowance trimmed and the markings adjusted as necessary. All seam lines and cross markings should be checked again to ensure the front and back pieces fit together neatly with the shoulder and side seams, and the bust, waist, hip and hem line.

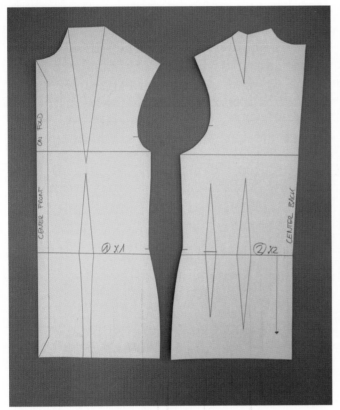

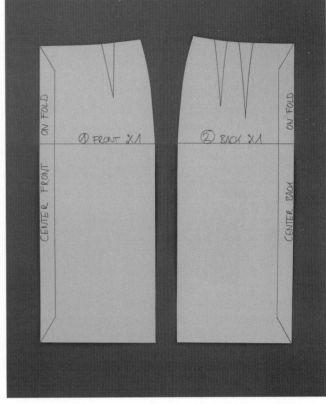

Then the fabric pieces can be transferred to paper. The basic patterns, created and cut out to be transferred almost directly from the mannequin to the body, are now ready. In comparison with the directions given for making up the patterns on pages 44 and 62, it is clear that the result is almost identical, but the procedure used to get there is very different. Obtaining the best results with each method depends on the model, the fabric and, above all, the personal preferences of the pattern designer.

Practical dressmaking tips

Fabric

The fabric used will also obviously have an influence on the pattern. Each fabric has its own properties specific to the material, which need to be taken into account when cutting and making up the garment. Woven and nonwoven fabrics and knits from various plant, animal and chemical sources differ in their appearance, strength, fineness and feel, in their stretchability and elasticity, moisture absorption, effect on the skin and moldability.

For instance, with thick and heavy materials it is sometimes necessary to have larger seam allowances, and avoid sharp angles or various seams converging in the same place. For stretch fabrics, particularly jersey, tighter patterns without any darts are often used. Such special cases, however, will not be looked at in depth here.

Nevertheless, it is always advisable to purchase the fabric before proceeding to draw the pattern, and to consider certain aspects and, wherever possible, try it out on a mannequin or in front of a mirror. How a fabric behaves – the way it hangs, its effect and volume – can mostly be learned with practical experience. Careful inspection of the original material (for example, the depth of the pleats in the cloth) will usually save us having to make a lot of alterations in the paper pattern later on.

Depending on the type of material, fabrics should be pre-washed, dampened or dry-cleaned before cutting, and treated in accordance with their natural properties during the sewing stage, since fabrics that have shrunk, stretched, or lost their shape can have quite a significant impact on the final result, as well as the cutting stage, requiring subsequent alterations in the pattern.

Cutting out

When cutting out, a few basic rules should be observed, since the aim is to use the least amount of material possible and minimize waste through fast and accurate cutting.

First of all, the right side of the fabric, i.e. the outside of the garment, should be determined. Then the material should be inspected for any flaws or irregularities. A check should also be made to see whether the pieces can be placed upside down, (i.e. turned top to bottom through 180°, not turned over), along the straight grain of the fabric. If, on the other hand, the fabric has a one-way design, such as a large floral print, or a nap running in a certain direction, like velvet, for instance, or corduroy, or a fabric with a different sheen or hue depending on the light, the pattern pieces should be laid out in such a way that they are aligned with the direction of the print or nap. When the garment is worn, it should be possible to brush the nap downwards, while prints should always run upwards.

Before cutting, the fabric should be ironed so as to anticipate any potential problems from contact with heat or steam, thereby guaranteeing a perfect cut. Fabrics that have lost their shape should be pulled square before cutting. For cutting purposes, the material is normally folded with the selvages together, so that the right side of the fabric is inside, and the pattern pieces can be traced on the wrong side with tailor's chalk. This will enable the pattern to be cut double and two identical, inverted pieces to be obtained (like mirror images) such as a right and left sleeve, for example.

The straight grain of the fabric runs parallel to the selvage, to which special attention should always be paid, since this will to a large extent be responsible for the perfect hang and fit of a garment. If the piece needs to be cut on the "bias", this should be done at an angle of exactly 45° to the straight grain of the fabric. When a fabric is cut on the bias, the pieces have more give and hang more softly, and are used primarily for dresses or bias binding. In many nonwoven fabrics, such as fusible interfacing, the pattern pieces can be placed in any direction.

With symmetrical pieces we often work with the so-called fold line, which means the cloth is folded in half with the pattern pieces being placed on top in such a way that the center line coincides with the fold. In this way, it is possible to cut out sym-

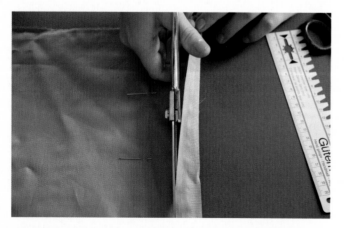

Special dressmaker's shears make cutting out much easier but should only be used to cut cloth. When cutting out, the lower scissor blade should glide directly over the table. Do not lift the fabric when cutting, otherwise the edges of the cloth may move slightly.

metrical pieces in two layers of cloth with both sides of the piece being absolutely identical.

Asymmetric pieces are not cut on the fold: they are cut on a single layer of cloth. Make sure that where pattern pieces are placed face down—they are placed on the wrong side of the fabric and not the right. The latter would produce a "mirror image" and result in the asymmetric shape hanging on the wrong side of the body.

In plaids or striped fabrics, the different layers should be pinned together with precision at certain points, or else all the pieces should be cut separately, so that they can be compared and the match points inspected. When making up these pieces, we recommend tacking them together first by hand, since they can easily slip if machined directly. When purchasing such fabrics, it should be borne in mind that a larger amount will be needed for the nap.

The fabric should be laid out flat on the table for cutting. To transfer the paper patterns to the fabric, they are first placed on the wrong side of the fabric and pinned in place. When using cardboard patterns or a material that cannot have pins inserted in it, the pattern pieces should be kept in place by means of weights. The pattern is transferred to the fabric, taking the seam allowances into account, by marking with chalk or a tracing wheel; or else the pattern is cut out directly on the cloth.

The cross markings, or construction symbols, which mark the point where the individual pieces should be sewn together, should be indicated by making small notches or marks, or by adding a few tailor's tacks by hand. It is very important that the markings and darts are traced identically on all layers of the fabric for pattern pieces that are cut double.

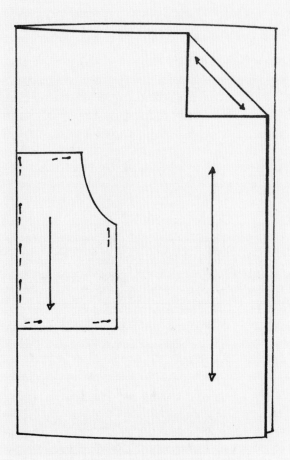

A woven fabric consists of lengthwise warp yarns, intersected by transverse weft threads. The raw edges are closed by the selvage. The width of the fabric depends on the loom, and is usually between 140 and 170 cm. Most woven fabric is sold in so-called bolts of cloth, and comes ready folded, i.e. with the selvages together.

Extreme care should be taken when working with printed or patterned fabrics. With plaids and striped fabrics, before the pattern pieces are laid out, the layers of cloth need to be placed exactly one on top of the other and held in place with pins. Another method is to lay all the pieces on the fabric separately, that is to say, neither one on top of the other nor placed on the fold line, and check the direction of the print along all the seams.

Seam allowances

In industrial dressmaking, seam allowances are usually included in the cardboard pattern pieces, so that the edges of the cardboard can be drawn or cut around directly. For tailoring, they are usually added to each cut, and then traced on the fabric with a tailor's square or using chalk and a measuring tape. The advantages of having set seam allowances are their low margin of error and the guarantee that each time the pattern is cut it will be identical.

A point in favor of patterns cut without seam allowances is that it makes it easier to inspect the pieces and join, measure and alter them, and that the width of the seam allowance can vary depending on the type of cloth used. Nevertheless, one of the drawbacks is that it takes a lot longer to cut out the pattern. The decision for or against leaving seam allowances in the pattern is left in the hands of the individual pattern maker, who will decide in light of their own experience, since both methods have their good and bad points. In any case, the distribution of the seam allowance will depend on the type of fabric, layout of the pattern, and sewing technique used. Broadly speaking, let's say we should add about 4 cm to the hem, between 1.5 and 2.5 cm to vertical seams and shoulder seams, and for narrower curved seams, such as those of the armhole and neckline, and on overlapping pieces such as the collar and pockets, about 1.5 cm. For the seams on sleeves and sleeve caps, 2 cm should be added. Pieces cut on the bias require larger seam allowances since they tend to give more when hung up. If necessary, the seam allowance can be trimmed or cut back in "layers" later on. This means that where two seam allowances converge, the inner seam should be cut much narrower than the outer seam, so that the edges do not lie directly on top of each other or exert pressure on the outside of the garment. In curved sections, the seam allowances should be eased in so that they can lie better on the curve.

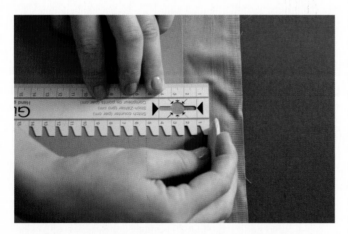

The seam allowances should be marked on the fabric with chalk or a special marker. For markings on the right side of the fabric, for example for the position of the pockets, there is a special type of chalk, which can be rendered invisible with a hot iron.

To neaten the seams, a serger can be used or else the edges can be finished with a zigzag stitch. With certain types of cloth and closed linings, it is sufficient to use pinking shears, which will stop the edges from fraying.

Pattern for the lining

For many garments a lining is recommended, either to improve its appearance inside, to enhance its thermal insulation, or else to make it more comfortable to wear. There are various types of lining, for example viscose, silk, synthetic fiber, and warm quilted linings. One of the common features of linings is their smoothness, to get the garment on and off with ease. For pockets, among other things, a thick cotton lining is generally used, which is much more stable.

The lining is generated from the basic pattern, after this has been tried on and completed, and requires a few minor alterations. This of course will depend mainly on the sort of finish required. For example, for garments with facings made from the outer fabric sewn to the front, sleeve and neckline, a decision will have to be taken as to exactly where and how to stitch the lining to the outer fabric. The facings should be omitted in the lining. A reduction in the number of seams, the solution of the hem line and the fold of the lining in the center back in jackets and coats are possibilities that need to be taken into account in accordance with the specific model.

As a basic rule, it can be said that the lining should always be cut a couple of millimeters wider than the pattern itself, to avoid any unattractive pulling even when the outer fabric needs to give a little. The lining should not be tight or interfere with the hang of the garment.

The inner lining is cut without any extra fabric for the hem, since it will always need to be shorter than the finished garment. Depending on the model, the lining is closed at the hem line of the garment (e.g. the majority of jackets). Serging the seam allowance is therefore not necessary in the case of most fabrics. It is also possible that the main fabric and its lining, which is a few centimeters shorter, will each need hemming separately, with the garment remaining open at the bottom, as is often the case with many skirt designs and a few coats. In this case, the seam allowances on both the main fabric and also the lining should be neatened to prevent fraying and ensure that the garment looks attractive. Usually, in thin slacks made of wool a lining is included at the front, which reaches down below the knee to avoid any bagging around the knees and hide the pocket seams.

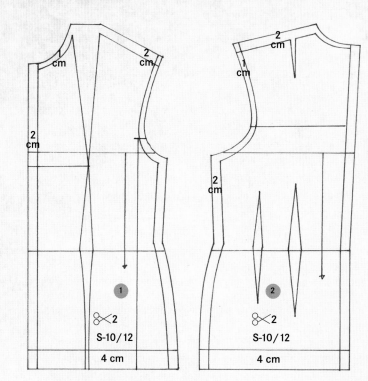

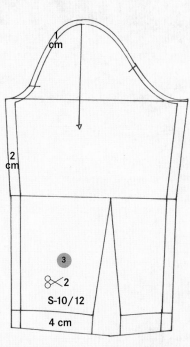

If the seam allowance is drawn on the pattern, its exact width should be stated. This will make it clear where the original cutting line (i.e. the stitching line) is, which is very important if any alterations need to be made. Accurate labeling of all the pattern pieces with the name of the model, serial numbering, straight grain, type and number of the piece and pattern size will make it easier to save and alter the pattern later on.

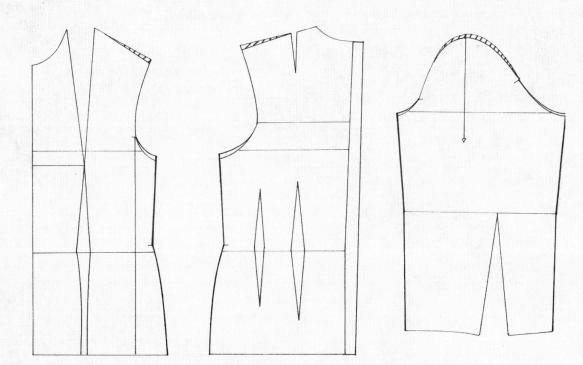

If shoulder pads are used, the shoulders and upper part of the sleeve in the cut for the lining should be flattened slightly, since, thanks to the shoulder pad, the roundness of the shoulder in the lining will not be as full as that of the main fabric. On the other hand, the cut for the lining should be increased in the underarm area, since the lining here needs to have more room to move.

Sewing the pattern pieces together

Sewing the pieces accurately with a sewing machine demands a certain amount of knowledge and experience of one's own machine. Both the so-called industrial and domestic sewing machines can be bought from stores. The former are larger and faster, specialize in just one type of stitch, and only work from the mains, whereas the latter often have several different stitching modes and are more appropriate for private use.

The sewing machine is normally used with the straight stitch, or lockstitch, as it is also known. The act of sewing pieces together is therefore often referred to as "stitching together". Before sewing the pattern pieces together, it is a good idea to try out a sample on a scrap piece of material that is the same as the one that will eventually be used. This will enable you to adjust the tension for the top and bottom thread, the strength of the cotton, the needle in the machine, the length and shape of the stitch, and check that they are appropriate for the type of fabric and for the purpose we have in mind. The fabric will always be sewn along the stitching line, and the distance from the edge of the cloth will be determined by the seam allowance selected in each case. Apart from basic sewing, we shall now explain how to do a few challenging seams to achieve a particularly pleasing result in garments that do not have a lining.

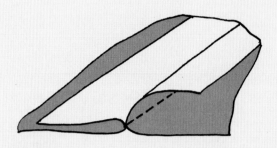

Flat seam
Most seams such as shoulder, divisional and side seams are sewn with a flat seam: two pieces of cloth are joined together by a straight line of stitches. The beginning and end of the seam should be secured by a couple of backstitches. This type of seam is normally neatened and pressed open.

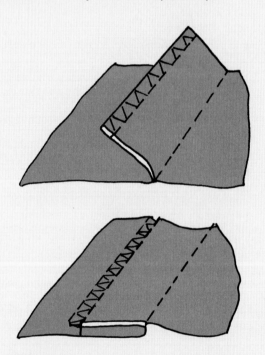

Folded seam
This is the preferred seam for heavy-duty areas such as the outer seams on jeans. For this folded seam both pieces of fabric are placed right sides together and the seam closed along the seam line. In the next step, the seams of both edges are put together and neatened, and then trimmed to the desired width.

Next, the seam allowances are folded over to one side and pressed. Then they are sewn up on the right side along the first line of stitching, at the same distance as the seam allowance. This will leave the reverse side of the seam and stitching visible on the right side of the fabric. Normally, if the seam allowances and darts have not been pressed open, they should be folded back to the center of the body and the side seams, so as to eliminate as much "bulk" as possible from the body.

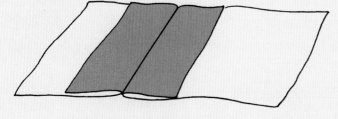

French seam

This is suitable for lightweight fabrics that are not lined, like tops for example, since from the outside it looks like a simple flat seam but has a really good seam inside. Both layers of fabric are sewn wrong sides together and the seam allowance is trimmed to between 0.5 and 1 cm. Before turning the garment the right way out, the seam is pressed open down the middle, so that it lies completely flat.

However, the layers are then folded over again, so that the seam allowances are encased inside. A second line of stitching is sewn on the wrong side of the fabric very close to the edge of the seam allowance. The seam allowance of the first seam remains encased and invisible inside the second seam: on the right side of the fabric the seam is flat, while it is also very neat on the wrong side.

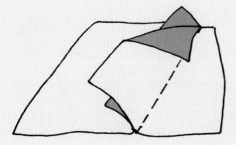

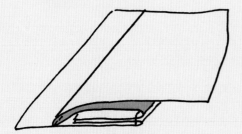

Flat-felled seam

The heavy-duty flat-felled seam is mainly used for pockets or double face fabrics (fabrics that consist of two materials of different colors that are joined together so that each side is a different color). First of all, the fabric is placed wrong sides together and stitched along the seam line. Then one of the two seam allowances is trimmed to 0.5 cm, with the other one remaining roughly twice this width.

Next the larger seam allowance is placed on top of the smaller one, pressed and turned over, and then topstitched on the right side close to the edge of the fabric. The narrowest seam allowance will be encased inside the seam and invisible, with the seam lying flat and neat on both sides of the fabric.

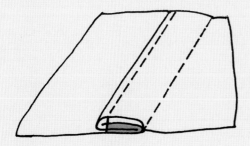

Hand-sewn seam

The seam sewn by hand using a needle, thread and thimble is almost never used on an industrial scale. However, in haute couture and bespoke tailoring, it allows hems, adjustments, appliqués, embellishments, etc to be done with greater precision. It can also make a subtle difference in ready-made garments.

It is important to use the appropriate needle and thread for the material in hand and to maintain the correct posture, not only with regard to the sewing tools used but also with respect to our own body. In work requiring lengthy periods of concentration, resting the work on a raised knee will make it easier on our eyes and back. Working with the thimble or finger pad on the middle finger of our sewing hand will probably take some getting used to at the beginning, but in the long run it will save us from continually pricking our finger as we push the needle head through the cloth. The thread should be secured with a small knot or invisible stitch at the beginning of the seam, and backstitched at the end. We shall now explain some basic hand stitches.

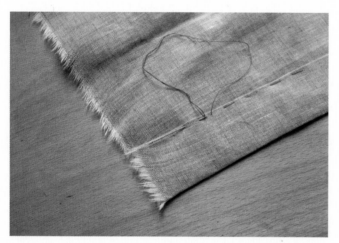

Basting or tacking

Basting or tacking is the simplest hand stitch of all, and in theory is only used to fix the material in place, for fitting the garment, or before proceeding to stitch the garment. It consists of making simple evenly spaced stitches each about 0.5 cm long. Of course, we will first have to check whether the fabric will take the stitch, and then baste outside the seam line. A special heavy-duty, easily breakable basting thread will help keep the material in place and will also make it much easier to remove later on.

For beginners, it may be particularly useful when sewing difficult parts such as a zipper for example, to baste the pieces before stitching them together. Rather than merely pinning in place, basting has several advantages and our effort is soon repaid. It stops the pieces from slipping or shifting position, and the garment can be tried on without worrying about being pricked by pins. The material can be ironed and manipulated, and it is not necessary to interrupt the stitching process to remove the pins.

Hem stitch

With a bit of practice it is possible to learn to sew an invisible hem by hand. To do so, the hem allowance is turned over once and neatened. Alternatively, it can simply be turned over twice instead, as in this example. The stitches are hidden slightly beneath the hem, or sewn directly on the edge of the fold from right to left. This means that only a few threads of the fabric are picked up by the needle from underneath the hem. On the right side the stitches should only be seen as tiny little stitches in the best of cases. The needle advances diagonally moving between the cloth and hem. The space between each stitch is about 6 mm. The thread is not pulled tight but left a bit loose, to stop it from breaking, and also to enable the tip of the iron to pass below the edge of the hem when pressing the garment.

Herringbone stitch

Herringbone stitch is used to hem stretch fabrics and thick materials and edges, which can get caught easily, such as trouser hems, for instance. It is more durable, and does not break when the fabric is pulled. This cross stitch is sewn from left to right, with each part of the stitch being oriented from right to left, that is to say, in the opposite direction. This gives the thread a certain amount of play, so that, if subjected to tension, it will be able to yield slightly. Therefore, the stitch begins on the left of the seam or else, in the case of round seams (e.g. at the bottom of the trouser leg) on the inner side of the side seam.

On the outer layer of material only one or two strands of thread are picked up from right to left, before the needle is passed diagonally beneath the hem and from right to left again. When the thread is pulled out again, the needle is passed upwards to the other side and once again inserted in the main fabric. Stitching continues by alternating between the hem and outer fabric. In this way, the edge of the hem will be hidden inside making it impossible for it to get caught later on. Like hem stitch, herringbone stitch should also be almost invisible from the outside.

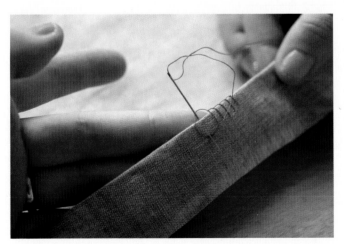

Buttonhole stitch

The stitch known as buttonhole stitch is used to make buttonholes by hand or to oversew raw edges. The stitches can be sewn so close together, if need be, that the vertical stitches lie side by side, as in the case of a buttonhole for example, or they can be set further apart, like a blanket hem. Buttonhole stitch is sewn from right to left. The needle is inserted from behind the cloth and the thread pulled through to the front, with the point of the needle passing through the loop. If the needle is pulled tight, the overlap of the thread should lie directly over the raw edge or end of the fabric.

Fitting

The fitting of a cut should always be done with great care, and even speed, since for the person doing the modeling it is very wearisome as they have to stand up straight and keep very still with their weight distributed on both feet. For this reason, the pieces for the fitting need to be properly prepared, that is to say, with all the pattern markings on them (bust, waist and hip line, front line of the sleeve, match points for the sleeve, center front and back), and should be tacked with sufficient seam allowance, or basted with long stitches. The piece to be fitted is normally prepared with a sample material that is less valuable but comparable in strength, and hangs in a similar way to the original fabric planned to be used, such as a fine cotton greige for a dress, for example, or a thick woolen fabric for a coat. Normally two fitting sessions are required, in which the second session is really just to check the alterations made after the first fitting. The pieces tried on during the fitting should be pinned together at the center front or back, starting at the waist and working your way up and down. At the neckline and curves in the sleeves, the seam allowances should be tucked in so that they do not get in the way when sewn up. The best thing is to stand in front of a mirror for the fitting, so that it is possible to get a general idea after each alteration is made merely by looking in the mirror.

First the width should be checked and, where necessary, adjusted by letting it out on the vertical seams, since if it is too tight, the garment will not hang right. To do this, the relevant seams should be undone and pinned together again on the person. Normally the width should be evenly distributed across the body, that is to say, the same amount of fabric should be let out or taken in on both side seams or stitching lines in the pattern, provided these do not involve any lopsidedness. The seams in the center front and center back will not be altered. The garment should then be checked for balance. The center front, center back and side seams should hang vertically over the hips, and the bust and hip lines should be horizontally aligned with the body. The width of the skirt hem should cover both legs equally.

Any deviations with respect to balance should be corrected to prevent the garment from "sagging". This should be done in the shoulder seams for tops and at the waistline in the case of skirts. If all the parts of the garment are well balanced, the shoulder seams should be carefully pinned together, with any extra material being taken in if the neckline is found to plunge too low, or the collar bone is too visible. The neckline should be checked for comfort.

The stitching lines between the different pieces and the width of the hem should be checked against the sketch of the pattern and adjusted as necessary. Curvatures for the bust, tummy, darts and hips should be given shape, always taking the center panels

as a reference. In other words, in a vertical seam, such as a princess seam (which extends from the shoulder over the bust right down to the hem), the sewing line (which lies on the center front or back) should be kept as straight as possible, with the shape being formed on the other side of the seam, and held together with pins. This makes the seams look straight.

As a general rule, puckering and diagonal pull denote sources of error. In most cases, the cause is an error involving the straight grain, uneven distribution of width, or a distance that is too short. When fitting a mounted collar, the collar is pinned from the center back round to the center front. Any corrections in the shape of the neckline should be made at this stage. The upper edge of the collar should cover the neck evenly.

Before inserting the sleeves, the shoulders and armholes should be seen to hang perfectly, and any annoying seam allowances should be tucked in. The armhole insertion match points should coincide with the insertion of the sleeve into the bodice and should be distributed evenly around the front and the back. Then the carefully prepared sleeve is placed on the arm, the seam allowances are turned inwards, and the insertion points are matched up and pinned together on the sleeve and bodice. Another pin is used to attach the sleeve to the shoulder point. The straight grain of the fabric, width and length of the shoulder should now be checked. The width should be distributed evenly between the pins on the sleeve insertion points and shoulder point. The movement of the sleeve, shoulder and armhole should be checked in the mirror. The sleeve should not rest on the upper arm but feel light and comfortable.

Any diagonal pull indicates an error, which can be solved by turning the sleeve or distributing the width more evenly. Any puckering on the shoulder suggests the height of the shoulder is too short, which means that the sleeve needs to be let out at the shoulder point. Wherever possible, the pins should be inserted perpendicular to the seam. Once the fitting is complete and the garment has been removed, the alterations should be marked in chalk or with colored thread and the cross markings put in. All alterations are transferred to the working pattern and the pieces that were tried on are altered for the second fitting. The collar and both sleeves should now be pinned on, so that attention can be turned to the position and entry point of the collar and sleeves in the second fitting.

The fitting session is a difficult stage in the creation of a pattern and requires sound preparation, patience, and eye training. Through practice and trial and error, we can gradually acquaint ourselves with this type of "sculpture" and learn to identify problems and their causes, and how to correct them and create better and better "shells" adapted to individual bodies. For a more thorough analysis, errors can be divided into five categories: errors that have arisen when taking measurements, flaws in the pattern layout, differences in shape that have gone unnoticed or not been taken into account, sewing errors (only sewn on one side, or pulled too tight, seam puckers, failure to consider the straight grain of the fabric, etc) and ironing defects (tightness, loss of shape, sheen).

Altering the shape of the pattern

Basic patterns which have been created by taking the measurements of the body usually have a good fit. However, in the majority of cases alterations are still necessary. Some of the alterations required are clear and are made once the pattern has been laid out and are made before the pattern is cut (for example, a disproportionately small or large bottom or tummy, raised or sloping shoulders, irregularities, such as lopsided shoulders, or one hip sticking out more than the other). Other differences only come to light at the fitting stage and therefore need to be adjusted afterwards. Another reason for carrying out alterations might be because of the changes that have occurred to the body with the passage of time, when a pattern that used to fit perfectly needs to be adjusted to fit the new measurements.

The paper pattern should be laid out flat and, where necessary, with all the creases being ironed out with a cool iron. Through the use of colored crayons or adhesive labels, the alterations will be clearer and attract our attention at first glance. An adhesive that does not dry immediately will enable you to make quick corrections. We should take into account that the pattern pieces usually must to be altered only in a half, or a quarter, of the actual amount since we are working with halves or quarters of the body circumference and the pieces will later be cut twice or on fold. However, this is obviously not the case with the sleeves. We shall now provide details of the most common alterations made to achieve a correct fit:

Alterations for a disproportionately large or flat tummy or bottom

Alterations for a flat tummy or a pronounced bottom are necessary when the measurements for the waist circumference (WAC) and hip circumference (HC) are very disproportionate. The difference in size can be detected simply by measuring. On the side line, the center front and center back should be measured perpendicularly from the waist line, marked with the tape measure, all the way down to the floor. In this way we will obtain the measurements for the length of the side, front and back. The difference between the front and back lengths and the side mea-

surements will indicate an abdomen that is larger than normal. In this case the rule is: front or back length + 1 cm = side length, since the contour of the hip requires one centimeter more (see instructions given for the basic skirt pattern on page 44, in which the waist line moves up 1 cm at the side seam). All differences with respect to this formula are an indication of how much the pattern pieces should be shortened or lengthened. These alterations are made on the basic pattern of the skirt or dress after the pattern has been made up. Of course the opposite may occur, that is to say, we may be faced with a larger tummy and smaller bottom. In this case, the procedure for making alterations is the same, except that it will need to be let out at the tummy and taken in at the bottom.

A simple example by way of illustration:
Side length: 105 cm
Front length: 103 cm (the normal measure would be: *side length % 1 cm*, that is to say 104 cm)
Back length: 105.5 cm (the normal measure would be: *side length % 1 cm*, that is to say 104 cm)
With a side length of 105 cm, the front length is measured as being 103 cm and the back length as 105.5 cm. Normally, the measurements for the front and back lengths should be about 1 cm less than the side length. This means that in this example the abdomen of the person measured is flatter (the front length is 1 cm shorter) and the back is slightly more pronounced (the back length is 1.5 cm longer) than in a "normal figure". To adjust the skirt to the body with these confirmed irregularities 1 cm should be snipped off the front length and 1.5 cm added to the back length.

1 To transfer the alterations to the basic pattern, on the front piece at the height of the tip of the dart a crosswise line should be drawn, and 1 cm further over another parallel line should be traced from the tip of the dart to the zero point on the side seam. It should be cut on both sides of the dart and along the upper crosswise line.

Likewise, on the back piece a horizontal line should be traced and cut at the height of the tip of the deepest dart. The sides of the darts should be cut open.

2 The upper crosswise line should be stuck to the lower line on the front piece so that 1 cm can be trimmed, or taken out. This will bring the two sides of the dart together. Paper should now be placed underneath the back piece of the pattern and the center back opened, or let out 1.5 cm. The pattern piece remains joined together at the side seam. It runs parallel on the center back as far as the dart and then slopes down towards the side seam. The

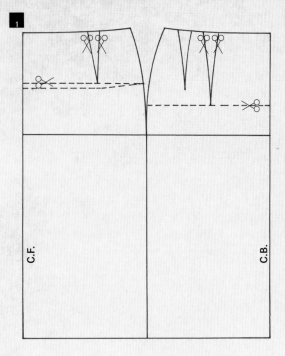

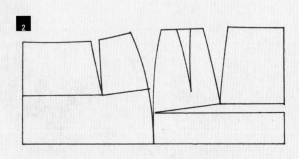

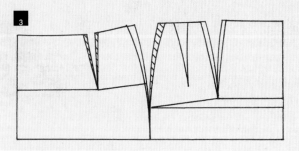

upper skirt piece should be stuck, thereby separating the two lines of the darts.

3 To finish, the legs of the dart that have been moved closer together at the front should be deepened just over 0.75 cm, and the width of 1.5 cm missing from the overall circumference should be added to the side seam. The new side seam feeds into the original seam at the level of the hips. On the other hand, 0.75 cm should be added to each side of the dart on the back. The extra width obtained on the back panel of the skirt should be removed from the side seam at the height of the hips.

Alterations in case of abnormally raised or sloping shoulders

4 The slope of the shoulders is calculated on the basic pattern by means of a formula. However, it does not always coincide with the actual shoulders. Neither is it uncommon for both shoulders to slope at different angles or to lean forward slightly. To correct a high shoulder, proceed as follows:

1 cm should be added to the front and back pieces at the outermost point of the shoulder. The new shoulder line runs towards the edge of the neckline. To avoid enlarging the armhole, the side seam should also be raised 1 cm under the arm, to enable the curvature to be distributed evenly and increased by 1 cm at the sleeve insertion point.

5 Unlike in the case of raised shoulders, to correct sloping shoulders 1 cm should be taken out both at the shoulder point and also on the side seam. The sleeve insertion points should then be moved down 1 cm. Both alterations can be made on the same side if necessary, and then two different front and back parts will need to be cut.

Altering a one-seam sleeve

After fitting it is often necessary to make alterations to the sleeves. For alterations deriving from a very large or very thin upper arm, a straight line should be traced and cut on the one-seam sleeve from the center of the sleeve hem to the center of the sleeve cap. The horizontal upper sleeve line should also be cut. Extra paper should be placed underneath the pattern piece. The pattern pieces should remain joined together at the shoulder and underarm points.

6 In the case of a large upper arm, the pieces of the sleeve are shifted outwards to the left and right so that they are lying 1 to 2 cm apart at the height of the upper arm line. There will thus be an overlap of the pieces along the horizontal upper arm line. By doing so, the sleeve cap is lowered without altering the size of the armhole, and the sleeve will be looser without any need to change the width of the sleeve pattern.

7 In the case of a thinner upper arm, the horizontal line is shifted above and below, so that the parts overlap along the vertical line in the pattern. The extra material is taken out where the parts merge. This gives a narrower sleeve with a higher sleeve cap, with the width at the top remaining the same. The bodice must not be altered in either case, since the extra width, that is, the additional width required in the sleeves with respect to the armhole, remains the same.

On the following pages we shall provide step-by-step instructions for creating basic skirt and top patterns. These can be used as a basic system for creative design and can be applied to each individual set of measurements. The examples derived from these models give us a general idea of the unlimited number of possibilities for varying the configuration of the pattern, and offer us some basic techniques for creative pattern making, showing us how to locate the lines of the design, for example, or how to proceed with darts, or how to insert pleats. Apart from the skills required for designing patterns, tips and tricks are also offered for implementing and completing the designs, such as, for example, how to sew in various types of zipper or pleats, as well as learning how to add a facing to a top.

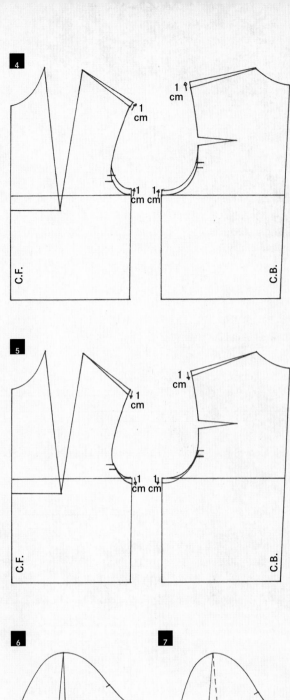

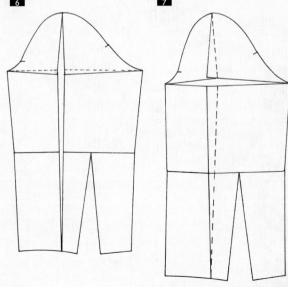

Basic pattern for a straight skirt

Most skirt models are based on the straight skirt block pattern. New variations can be implemented, for instance by subdividing into several panels, i.e. with seams, the insertion of godets, shortening or lengthening the total length, or altering the height of the waistline. The basic skirt pattern should always be straight and fitted at the waistline. This makes it possible to create a perfect fit: alterations can be made without any problem and proportions are easier to calculate. The waist circumference, which is smaller than that of the hips (the widest part of the body), is obtained by reducing the measurements at the waistline.

Sample measurements

WAC Waist circumference 68 cm – 34 cm
HC Hip circumference 98 cm – 49 cm
HD Hip depth 20 cm
SKL Skirt length 60 cm

Calculated sample measurements

1/2 WAC Waist circumference (34 cm) + *1 cm width allowance* = 35 cm
1/2 HC Hip circumference (49 cm) + *1 cm width allowance* = 50 cm
Intake (difference between HC and WAC) = 15 cm
Darts intake calculation: side seam: 7 cm, front panel: 2.5 cm, back panel: 5.5 cm

The difference between the waist and hip circumference is known as intake. Depending on the shape of the body and skirt model, the intake calculation will vary on the front and back panels and will often need to be altered in the fitting room.

1   **4**   **5**

Waistline

Hipline

2

C.F.   Side Seam   C.B.

Hem

3   **6**   **7**

1 - 2: The basic pattern begins on the front half of the skirt, where point 1 is defined. Point 2 is obtained by tracing a 20-cm vertical line (the hip depth), from this point straight down towards the hem.

1 - 3: Starting at point 1, trace along this line to obtain the skirt length (60 cm), which will give you point 3. This length can be shortened or lengthened at will later on. Departing from all three points (1, 2 and 3), lines are traced at a right angle towards the right.

1 - 5: Then the waistline (half hip circumference of 49 cm + *1 cm seam allowance*) is drawn out from point 1. This will give us point 5.

5 - 7: In order to find the fold line in the back panel, trace another line the length of the skirt from point 5. The pattern should then be laid on the fold in the fabric to coincide with this line.

4 - 6: The reference for the side seam is obtained by halving the distance between points 1 – 5. This gives us point 4. Point 6 is obtained by following the same procedure as for point 3. Then a line is traced to join up the two points (4 and 6). The resulting rectangle on the left will become the front panel of the skirt, with the right side forming the back panel.

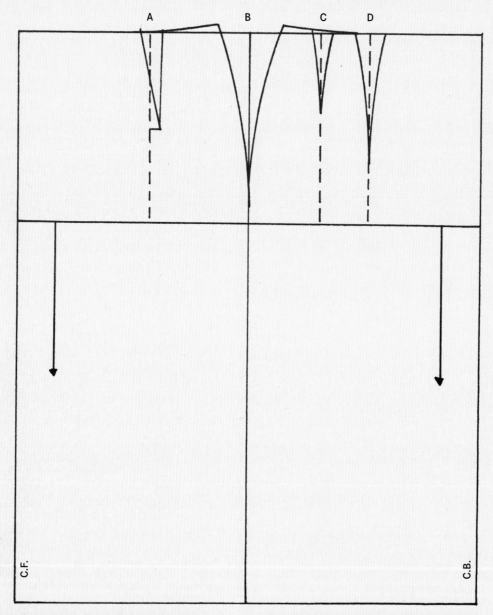

In order to fit the shape of the straight skirt to the body, the next step is to adjust the intake measurements to the waistline. In accordance with the darts intake calculation, remove a total of 7 cm on the side seam, 2.5 cm at the front, and 5.5 cm at the back. On the back a dart measuring 3 - 4 cm should be ample. Where greater intake is required, this should be distributed between two darts as shown in the following example. To make the appropriate darts, proceed as follows:

For dart A (*at a distance of 6 to 8 cm from the side seam*) allow a total of 2.5 cm. *The length* should be *between 9 and 11 cm*. It is advisable to move the tip of the dart *1 cm to the right* in order to achieve the best fit.

For dart B, allow 7 cm, that is, 3.5 cm on each side. The curve of the side seams should be traced in line with the contours of the body, and should re-enter the straight seam no further down than the hip height (line 2).

Dart D is located halfway between the side seam and the fold line. Remove 3 cm from the width and *14 to 15 cm from the length*.

Dart C is located right between the side seam and dart D, with a width of 2.5 cm and a *length of 12 to 13 cm*.

The baseline should be *raised 1 cm* at the side seam and *0,5 cm* at the next two darts (A and C) so as to follow the contours of the body. The waistline is now marked and rounded. The darts on the back (C and D) should be slightly convex in shape, so as to fit the contours of the body adequately.

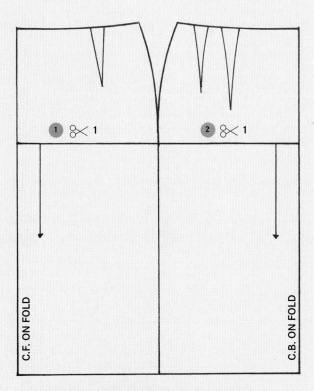

The front and back of the skirt should now be separated. The hip curve is marked on the side seam with the French curve, and then follows the contours of the body before returning to the straight side seam at a point no lower than the hipline. This curve often needs to be altered in the fitting room.

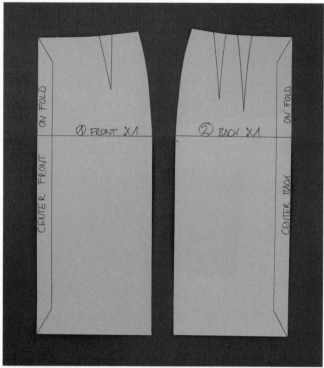

The prepared parts of the pattern should be cut out along the straight grain of the fabric:

1️⃣ Skirt front, 1x on the fold

2️⃣ Skirt back, 1x on the fold

For the first fitting of the basic skirt, which mainly consists of a sample fabric, there should be a generous seam allowance (about 3 cm at the side seams), with the darts and side seams being tacked together with long stitches.

Sew from the waistline to the hem along the right side. On the left side, leave the seam open above the hipline, to enable the skirt to be tried on. The seam is then pinned together to fit the body.

The seams should not be oversewn at the beginning or the end, so that they can be ripped apart easily. Where major alterations are required, for instance, on account of a mistake in the measurements, it should be possible for these to be made as quickly and simply as possible.

During the first fitting, care should be taken to ensure that the waistline coincides horizontally with the smallest part of the upper half of the body, and that the side seams always run straight down the sides of the body. Finally, the darts should be examined and, where necessary, reduced or further darts added. For example, in the case of a larger tummy, it may be necessary to insert two darts in the front of the skirt.

If the skirt has been tried on and the cut is perfect, it can also be sewn up without any alterations as a basic model cut from the main fabric. In such cases, the seam allowance on the finished skirt should not be wider than 2 cm; otherwise it might pull on the hip circumference and bunch up. A zip should be sewn into the left side seam, which should be open to the hipline. It is of course also possible to insert another closure in the front or back panel and vary the length. For the hem an allowance of 4 cm is recommended. This can also be topstitched 2 cm from the bottom on the outer side of the garment. Alternatively, the hem can also be turned up 4 cm, pressed and invisibly stitched by hand.

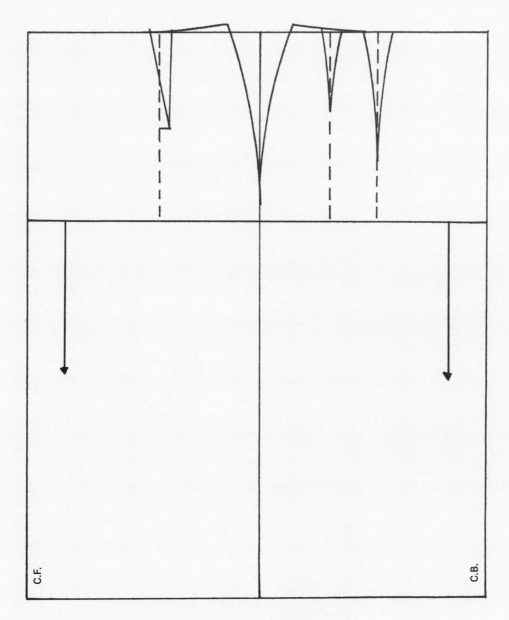

The basic skirt pattern drawn to a scale of 1:4

A-line skirt with yoke and side pocket variation

This model shows how a new silhouette can be created by letting out the hem line on the basic straight skirt pattern. The waistband and sophisticated pocket solution are further details that can help improve the classic skirt shape. So as not to affect the graphic line of the skirt, an invisible zipper is sewn into the left side seam. Its special feature is that no stitches can be seen on the outside of the garment, with only a smooth seam and the zipper pull of the fastener being visible. Step-by-step instructions on how to insert an invisible zipper are given in the annex.

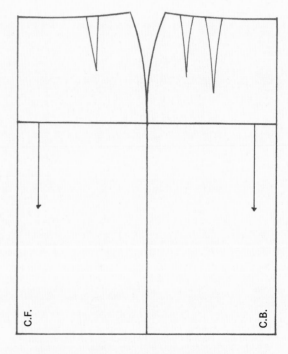

The basic straight skirt pattern can be used as a basis for this skirt. Since this is a symmetrical model, the basic skirt pattern is folded in half, and the center front and center back are aligned with the fold in the material.

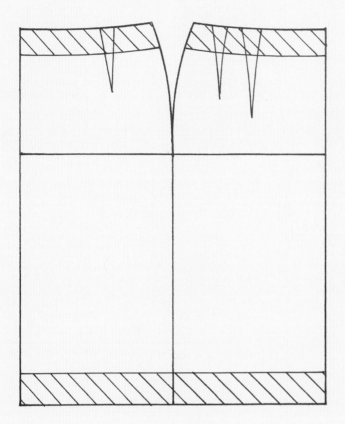

In keeping with the design, certain alterations need to be made to the basic cut at the beginning: the upper edge of the waistband should be moved down about 4 cm, so that the skirt has a slightly lower waist line. The hem is shortened 5 cm following the model.

For the slightly flared shape of the skirt, the side seams on the front and back sections are widened 3 cm at the hem. The new side seam line returns to the original line at the level of the hips. So that the hemline is still straight after the pieces have been sewn together, when cutting out the pattern make sure that the new section forms a right angle with the aid of a tailor's square.

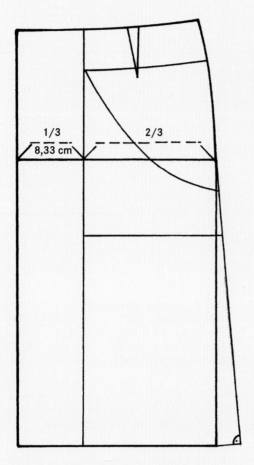
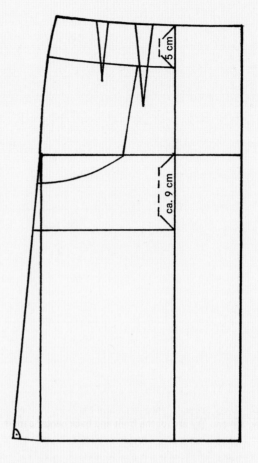

We shall now describe how to draw the basic construction lines of the pattern: the design of the front and back panels is arranged in three sections each of the same width. In order to determine the width of these sections, the following calculations should be made: the width of half of the pattern on the hip line (50 cm) should be divided into three, giving 16.66 cm. A line is traced from the front or back of the side seam, with just one of the sections being evened to a width of 8.33 cm, since the pattern is cut with both the front and back sections being placed on the fold line. In other words, they are laid on the fold of the fabric and cut double.

On the side pieces, going down from the new edge of the waist line, in accordance with the design, draw the waistband with a width of 5 cm. The respective middle section runs from the waist line down to the hem.

To make the side pocket, first trace the pocket opening, with the construction lines being drawn out according to the design. In this example the deepest point is at the height of the side seam. 20 cm can also be measured from the new waistline down on

the side seam. The front section is curved right round to the point at which the waistband intersects with the front center panel. At the back, the section is curved to a freely determined point. In this case, they were measured at a distance of 10 cm from the side seam and taken down to the hip line. This new point is then continued in a straight line to the seam of the waistband.

The side panels of the skirt will subsequently come to an end on this line, so as to accommodate a pocket opening. The pocket facing, which cannot be seen from the outside, starts on this line and should be given a lower border, which is known as the pocket depth. This is where it comes to an end, approximately 9 cm below the hip line. The limits of the pocket on the sides are defined by the vertical seam lines down the center sections on the front and back panels. For the pocket extensions, in other words the side panels covering the hips above the opening, the same lines are used. This enables both parts (the pocket and its extension) to be joined together horizontally and vertically on the center panel.

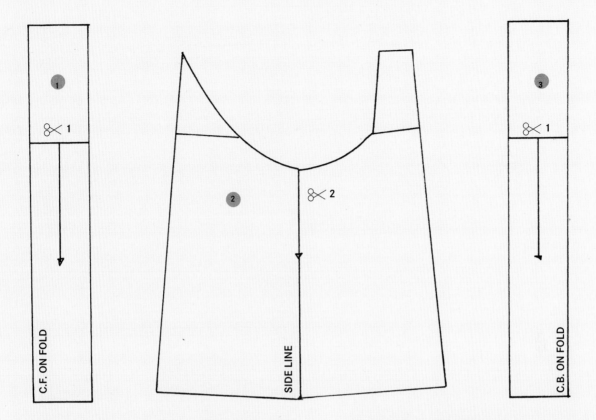

We can now proceed to trace the individual pieces of the pattern. Pieces 1 and 3 are for the front and back center panels. As can be seen in the photo of the finished skirt, the side pieces for the pockets are formed by a continuous piece of material joined to the front and back panels. The side pieces are thus joined together on the side seam to obtain piece 2 of the pattern, so that they fuse together to form a single piece.

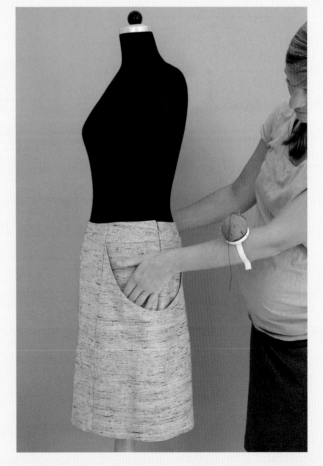

For the facings it is advisable to prepare a continuous band, which is laid out on the center front and back on the fold line (pieces 9 and 10). So as to make the skirt more comfortable to wear, without inserting any more seams (which would only make it look too bulky), the darts can be removed. The line of the darts can also be trimmed and the excess fabric taken out. The waistband is curved as the parts are joined together again, with their edges being evened up with the French curve. The photo illustrates how the inner waistband (10) of the back panel is put together. For the front panel the same procedure is followed, although here only one dart should be removed.

The next step is to assemble the pieces for the waistband (4 and 5) using the waistband interfacing without any darts as a guide. These should be traced up to the line marking off the middle section. At this point they are sewn together with the sections in the front and back panels.

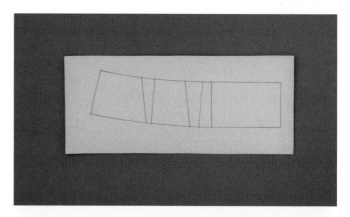

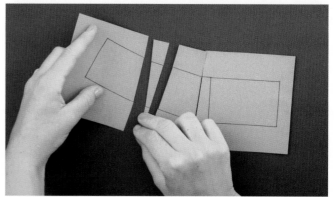

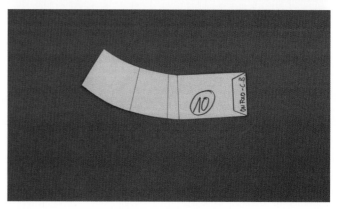

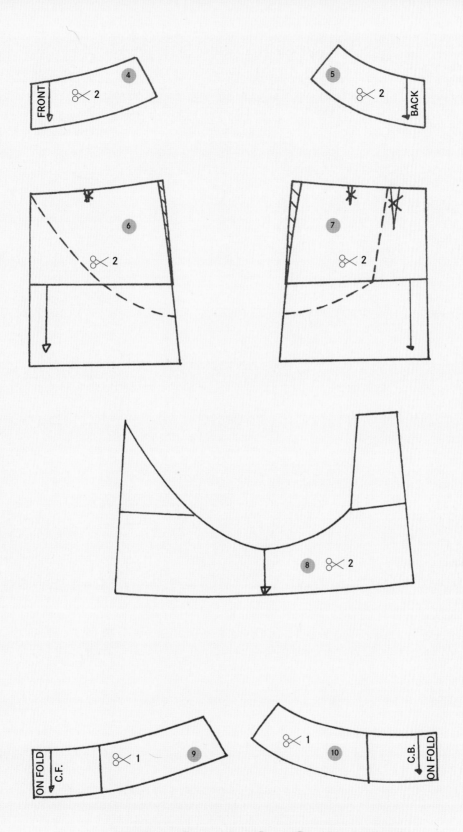

Pieces 4 and 5, along with 9 and 10, are now finished. The upper side pieces 6 and 7, which form the pocket extension, should be traced so that they reach as far as the line marking the pocket depth. The remaining small tips of the darts should be taken up in the side seam, since they are too small to be sewn. Piece 8 is the pocket facing or overlay, which is joined together on the side seam of the paper pattern to become just one piece.

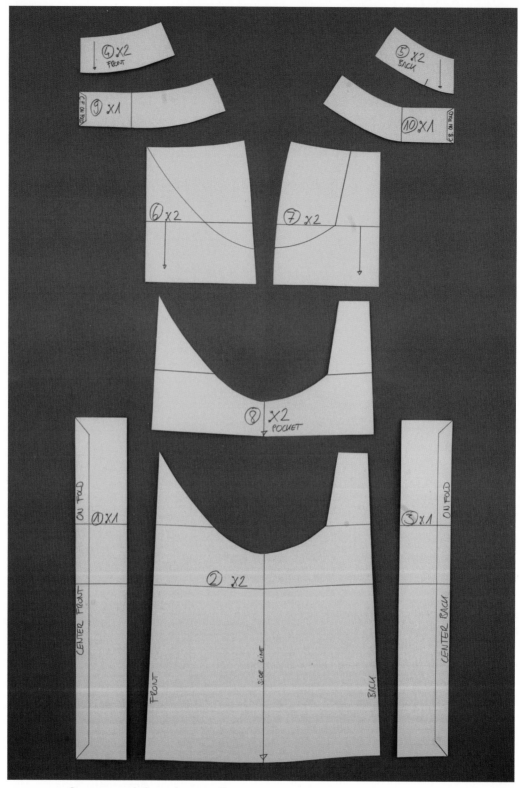

Once prepared, these pieces are then
cut out as follows:

1 Center front panel, 1x on fold line   6 Front side piece, cut 2

2 Side piece, cut 2   7 Back side piece, cut 2

3 Center back panel, 1x on fold line   8 Pocket facing or overlay, cut 2

4 Front waistband, cut 2   9 Front yoke, 1x on fold line

5 Back waistband, cut 2   10 Back yoke, 1x on fold line

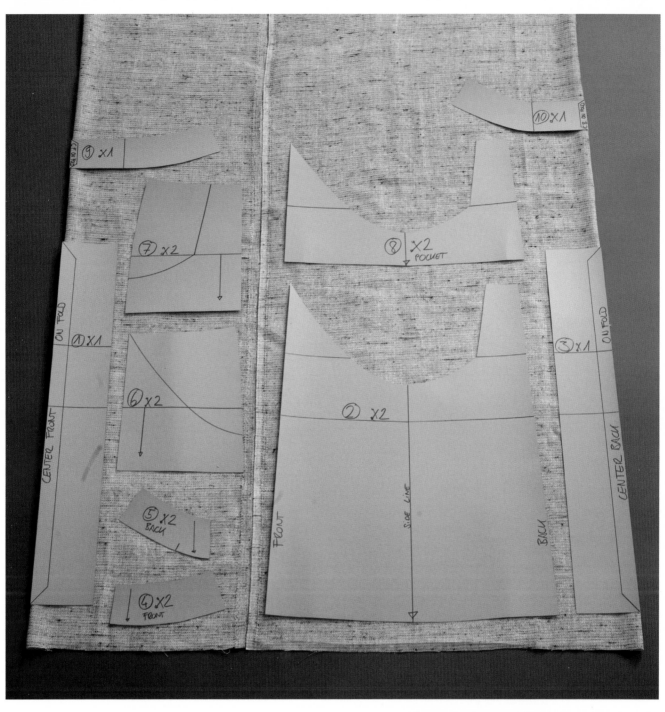

The way the pieces are laid out always depends on the width of the fabric. In this case, the material is folded about a third of the way across. This will give us 2 fold lines, leaving sufficient space to cut out the widest piece of the pattern. All pieces should be laid out and cut on the straight grain of the fabric. It is recommended that the standard seam allowance should be no less than 1.5 – 2 cm in the longitudinal seams, 1 – 1.5 cm in the curved seams, and 4 cm at the hem.

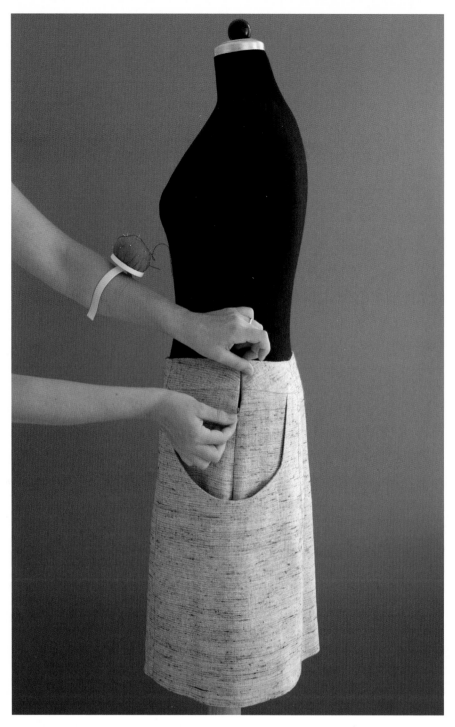

The invisible zipper is sewn into the left side seam. Its special feature is that no stitches can be seen on the outside of the garment, just a smooth seam and the zipper pull. The easiest way to do this is to sew the zipper into the pocket facing first, before sewing it to the remaining skirt pieces. In order to be able to get the skirt on and off easily, it should always be possible to open the zipper to the widest part of the body, which in this case is the hip line. For best results, a zipper that is a few inches longer should be used. There is a special zipper foot on the sewing machine to sew the zipper into place.

Depending on the fabric and preparation (e.g. pieces that do not have a lining) a few helpful tips might come in handy. Thus, it might be helpful, for instance, to strengthen this section with a 3 cm wide strip of interlining to make the fabric stiffer and to prevent stretching. Otherwise, the edges should be neatened to stop them fraying. Step-by-step instructions are given below for sewing in an invisible zipper.

First of all, the outer waistband is stitched to the side pieces, and the front and back side panels (6 and 7) are joined together up to a certain point. This means that the lower part of the seam up to the hip line is closed and sewn up tightly. The seam can also be basted with large stitches from the hip line up to the waist line, the seam allowances pressed open and then unpicked again up to the point where the zipper is inserted at the level of the hips. The ironed edges serve as a good guide to help sew the concealed zipper into place.

The fabric should be laid out right side up. The zipper is opened and placed with the front piece underneath on the right side of the fabric —starting at the top left-hand side, on the front side piece of the pattern. The teeth should be perfectly aligned with the anticipated sewing line, and the zipper tapes lying on the seam allowance. Now sew the zipper into place keeping as close as possible to the teeth.

Approximately 3 mm before reaching the beginning of the side seam, work the zipper towards the inner seam allowance and then continue to stitch for about another 2 cm, keeping within a space of 2-3 mm from the side seam to the seam allowance. This will allow for a full transition from the side seam to the zipper.

The zipper pull will subsequently be pulled through the gap created by sewing up both sides of the zipper. Finally, backstitch to finish off.

Then the zipper is closed and pinned in place on the right on the other side of the fabric. The ends of the two pieces of fabric and the intersecting seams of the waistband must of course meet at the same height. Then turn inside out and pin the zipper from the back so that it can be stitched to the seam allowance.

The zipper is then opened again, the piece is turned 180°, and then sewn up on the other side from bottom to top, keeping as close to the teeth as possible. As with the first side, start sewing about 2 cm below the side seam and stitch to within a few millimeters of the seam on the seam allowance.

When both sides of the zipper have been sewn, the zipper pull should be pulled up through the existing small hole in the side seam and the zipper secured on the wrong side beneath the stitching by a few horizontal stitches, and trimmed as necessary.

The invisible zipper is now finished. The pocket facings (pieces 6 and 7) can now be sewn together underneath the pocket overlay (piece 8) and this piece to the insertion line in the side panel (piece 2) of the skirt. They are then both accommodated in the main panels with the front and back center panels (pieces 1 and 3) so as to form the pocket itself.

The outer waistband pieces (9 and 10) are joined to the right side seam, with the left side remaining open, since the skirt has already been closed on this side with the zipper. The yoke pieces are then sewn right sides together to the edge of the skirt waist. The seam allowance of the waistband is folded inwards and thus hidden from view. The facings can be sewn by hand to the seam allowance inside or else topstitched by machine to prevent them from coming loose. The hem of the skirt can be stitched by hand or machine.

Basic pattern for tops and dresses

This basic pattern forms the basis for tops and dresses and is often used as an initial basic pattern for jackets and coats. It hugs the body and stretches from the neckline to the hip line. So as to avoid creating a "second skin" rather than a shell wrapping around the body, do not forget to add the following allowances to the measurements (see page 17). It is possible to generate an almost infinite number of variations of the model by making further alterations. In addition to this basic pattern for the bodice, explanations are also given for the pattern for the classic set-in sleeve with a dart. This forms the basis for all further sleeve variations.

Example for size 12/14

BC Bust circumference 92 – 46 – 23 – 11.5 cm
WAC Waist circumference 72 – 36 – 18 cm
HC Hip circumference 100 – 50 cm

N Neck (*1/10 of 1/2 BC + 2 cm*) 6.6 cm
BAH Back height 20.5 cm
BL Back length 41.8 cm
HD Hip depth 62.6 cm
BD Bust depth 28.9 cm
FL Front length 45.9 cm

Allowance

BAW Back width 17 cm
AD Armhole diameter (*1/8 BC % 1.5 cm*) 10 cm
BW Bust width (*1/4 BC % 4 cm*) 19 cm

BAH Back height + *1 cm* = 21.5 cm
BAW Back width + *0.5 cm* = 17.5 cm
AD Armhole diameter + *1.5 cm* = 11.5 cm
BW Bust width + *1.5 cm* = 20.5 cm
1/2 BC Bust circumference 46 cm + *3.5 cm* = 49.5 cm
(BAW + AD + BW = 46 cm)
SW Shoulder width 12.4 cm + *0.5 cm* (allowance for the back width) = 12.9 cm SW in front
+ *0.6 cm* (intake width) = 13.5 cm SW in the back
ABC Angle of bust dart: 16°

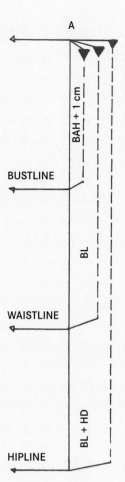

A

The tracing of the basic pattern begins with a vertical line, from the apex (A) at the base of the neck down the back height (including the extra allowance), the back length and the hip depth, forming a sloping line towards the left. This will give us the bust line, waist, and hip line.

BUSTLINE

BAH + 1 cm

BL

WAISTLINE

BL + HD

HIPLINE

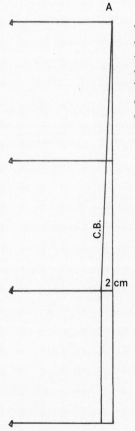

A

We will now trace the curvature of the spine, keeping within *2 cm* of the centre back (the vertical line) and tracing down to the waist line and then drawing a vertical line over the hips down towards the hem. Then going back up to rejoin the point at the base of the neck. This line gives us the seam line for the centre back.

C.B.

2 cm

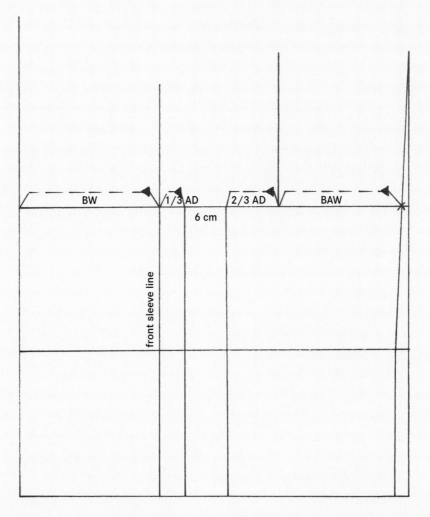

Starting from this point, where the line along the centre back and that of the bust line intersect, measure firstly the back width towards the left and trace an upward sloping line from this point. Then remove *2/3 of the armhole diameter* towards the left along the bust line and draw a sloping line from this point to the hem. This line will later be used to position the side seam of the back panel correctly.

There should now be a gap, of somewhat arbitrary dimensions, although never smaller than *6 cm*, so that later there will be enough paper available to separate the front and back pieces from each other without any problem.

Also on the bust line is the *remaining third of the armhole diameter*, with the vertical line here being the so-called front sleeve line. Next we trace the bust width, which will give us the center front.

A pause should now be taken to carry out some test measurements just to make sure. Half the bust circumference including the seam allowance without leaving any space should measure 49.5 cm in this case.

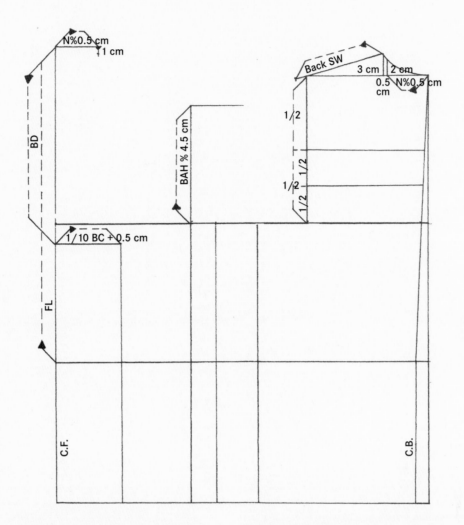

The line of the back width, together with the center back, the line for the back height, and the line for the base of the neck, forms the back panel. Once the shape formed by the sloping lines is complete, we will begin to form the back of the neckline, in which we measure from the base of the neck on the pattern of the *neck % 0.5 cm*, that is to say about 6.1 cm to the left, and trace a *2 cm* long line to the top.

A further *0.5 cm* is shifted over to the left, and then a parallel line measuring *3 cm* is traced—this is where the neckline back begins, which is drawn with the French curve.

The back shoulder width line also starts at the same point as the beginning of the neckline, with its length being traced through the point on the back panel. Care should be taken to ensure that the back shoulder seam is 0.6 cm longer than the one at the front. The extra width will be maintained when the garment is sewn together, ensuring a better fit at the shoulders.

Dividing the back panel horizontally in half will give us the subsequent position of the dart; a quarter of the way along is the back sleeve insertion point.

For the front shoulder width a line is drawn for guidance, in which the value of the *back height % 4.5 cm*, which is 17 cm in this case, is measured vertically to the top along the front sleeve line, at which point an auxiliary line of *10 cm approximately* is traced towards the right.

On the center front a measurement is taken from the waist upwards, tracing a straight line in a right angle with the measurement of the *neck % 0.5 cm*, before moving down another *1 cm* from this point onward. This is the point where the neckline and the left side of the bust dart meet.

Likewise, the bust depth is measured from top to bottom on the center front and angled *1/10 of the bust circumference + 0.5 cm* towards the right to obtain the bust apex.

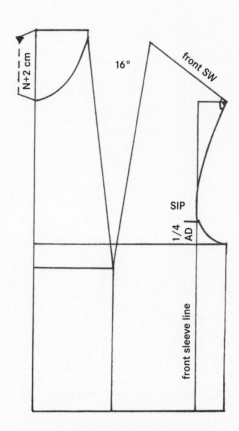

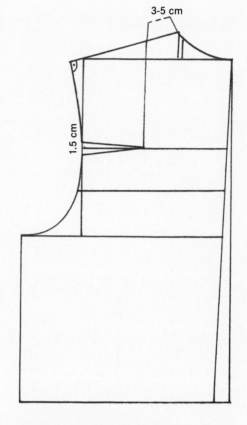

The front neckline is obtained by measuring the *neck + 2 cm* from the highest point on the center front to the bottom before curving round the neckline towards the reference point.

The left leg of the bust dart is taken to the bust apex, with the corresponding *angle* depending on the garment size (in this case, 16°) being subtracted and added to the right leg of the dart to make it the same length.

The front shoulder width of 12.9 cm is then made to meet the sloping line that serves as a reference for marking the armhole. The measurement *1/4 of the armhole diameter* is taken on the front sleeve line from the bust line to the top, which will give us the marking for the front sleeve insertion point (SIP).

On the back piece it is measured *3 – 5 cm on the shoulder line extending from the apex of the neckline*. From this point a perpendicular line is traced along the line marking half the back height. This is the point where the dart with a depth of *1.5 cm*, which is now marked on the back of the armhole, comes to an end. The armhole is now rounded off. Care should be taken to ensure that both shoulder lines converge at a right angle with the curve of the armhole; otherwise they will pucker into an unsightly crown when the pieces are sewn together.

The neckline-shoulder part of the pattern is now finished –the overall basic pattern is put together following the bust circumference measurements.

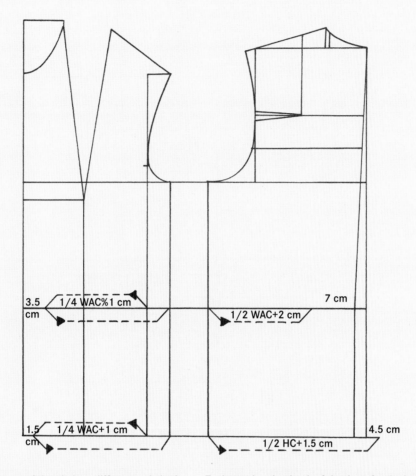

To take account of the obvious differences in body curves, darts can be added to reduce the waist line, or extra volume added to fit the contours of the hips. In order to calculate the depth of the darts, the following measurements should be taken into account:

Trace a line *1/4 of the waist circumference % 1 cm* towards the left along the waist line on the front piece, starting at the front sleeve line and measure the remaining amount to the center front. The corresponding difference, which in this case is 3.5 cm, will give us the depth of the dart.

The size of the dart on the hip line is determined by adding *2 cm to the result of the formula for the waist* (or *1/4 of the waist circumference + 1 cm*). This comes to 19 cm. The remaining amount to the center front is therefore 1.5 cm.

To determine the depth of the darts for the back, the value is used for *1/2 of the waist circumference + 2 cm* on the waist line from the outer left point just calculated towards the right and the amount still remaining to reach the back center line is measured, which in this case is 7 cm. On the hip line *1/2 of the hip circumference + 1.5 cm* is added from the point already calculated (in this case, 1.5 cm from the center front) to the right. This brings us to the center back of the basic pattern, with an extra amount of 4.5 cm, which needs to be added to the hip line. When measuring the waist and hip line, the gap in the middle, which is not measured, should be taken into account.

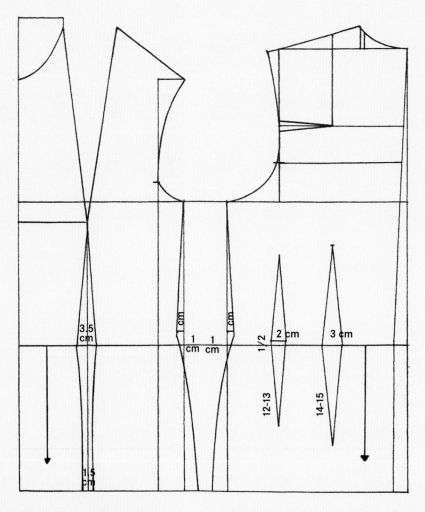

It is now possible to see the distribution of the excess fabric and location of the darts. The dart on the front piece lies on the line beneath the bust point and has a depth of 3.5 cm at the waist line and 1.5 cm at the hips. The dart is slightly rounded from the waist line down so as to fit the increasingly convex shape of the body properly.

The dart intake in the back section, which in this case is 7 cm from the waist line, is distributed on both side seams (each measuring 1 cm) and taken up by two darts. This helps the pattern fit the contours of the body properly and ensures that the

back darts are not deeper than 3 cm, which would hamper the correct fit of the garment. The extra width, which in this case is 4.5 cm, is added to both side seams (hence the distance between the front and back pieces) on the hips and curved into the waist line.

The waist line is raised 1 cm at the side seam, since the hip curvature requires a slightly greater length (see the basic skirt pattern on page 49). The next dart at the back is located at the lowest point, 0.5 cm above the original waist line.

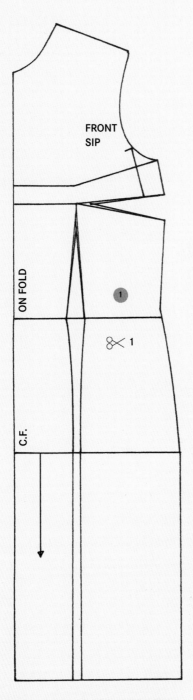

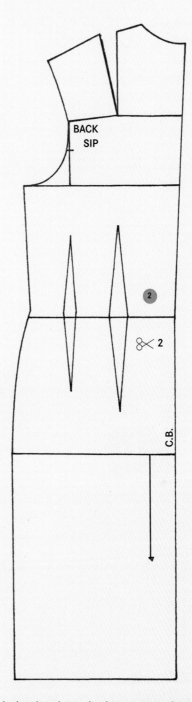

Where necessary, the length of the basic skirt cut can be extended from the hip line. It is advisable to insert the back armhole dart in the shoulder and the front bust dart in the side seam, since the seams look better there and are also less troublesome when further work is done on the pattern (e.g. working on the collar).

The bust and waist darts in the front section should always be shortened *about 2 cm* before cutting, to prevent them finishing right on the bust point.

This drawing shows the dress pattern piece ready for cutting. When relocating seams and darts, it should be noted that the further away from the original position, the greater the risk that the garment will not fit properly.

Basic sleeve pattern

The basic pattern for the sleeve is a classic sleeve with one seam. It can be used as a basis for almost all types of sleeve such as for example two-seam sleeves, raglan sleeves and batwing sleeves, even though the final sleeve often has very little in common with the original shape. Since it is a movable model, which means it should not ride up either in movement or when hanging down by the side, its correct position and machining is a bit tricky and requires some practice.

Example for size 12 / 14

SL Sleeve length 60 cm
SHH Sleeve head height (*BAH Back height % 6 cm*) 15.5 cm
SLW Sleeve width (*AD Armhole diameter + 5 cm*) 16.5 cm
SHW Sleeve hem width 23 cm
BAH Back height (20.5 cm + *1 cm*) 21.5 cm
AD Armhole diameter + *1.5 cm* = 11.5 cm

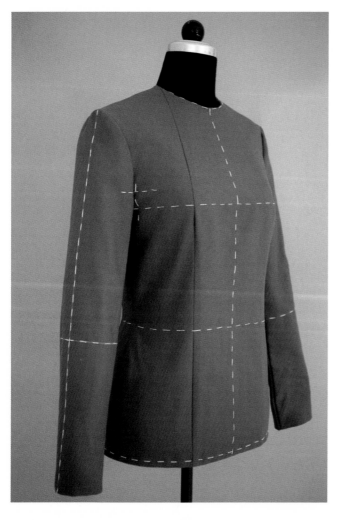

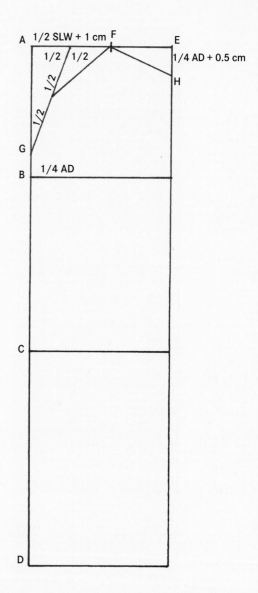

First of all, draw a vertical line measuring 60 cm down to the bottom. This line defines start point A and end point D, and marks the sleeve length. The sleeve head height is now traced from point A to obtain point B.
The distance between B and D is now halved and this section reduced to 2 cm (*1/2 B - D % 2 cm*) thus giving us the reference for elbow line C.

Starting from A again, trace a line to the right for the sleeve width to obtain point E. Halfway along this section *A – E + 1 cm* is the highest point of the sleeve (point F), which joins the shoulder seam of the bodice when the sleeve is inserted.

A vertical line is then traced to the top from point B *1/4 of the armhole diameter* and calculated to mark the front sleeve insertion point (point G). Another guideline (H) is obtained by tracing a vertical line downwards from point E for the value of the *armhole diameter + 0.5 cm*.

To obtain the start point on the left seam of the sleeve, trace a horizontal line from point B *1/3 of the armhole diameter* towards the left. Starting at this new point, measure the width of the sleeve **× 2**, the sleeve circumference, moving to the right, to obtain the start point for the right seam of the sleeve. Vertical lines are now drawn from both points to the hem line. Then the curved lines of the sleeve head are correctly marked in accordance with the three points created for guidance.

From the upper sleeve insertion point (point F) trace a line to guide point H. Divide it in half and then mark a subsequent point *1 cm* on the line.

Point J is determined by halving section A – F. It is then joined up to the front insertion mark (G) and then the section is halved once again. The corresponding point K is then joined up to sleeve insertion point (F) and raised *1 cm* at the halfway point (L).

Starting at point H, trace a line to the right side seam. When this is divided into three, it will give us start points M and N for both of the last reference points. At each sloping line *1 cm* (M) or *1.5 cm* (N) is now subtracted at a right angle and then the sleeve head curvature is marked with the French curve.

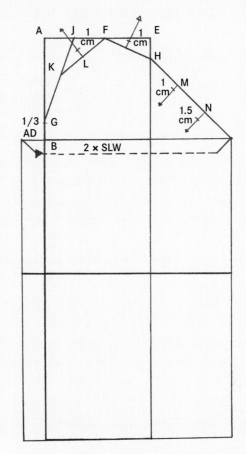

The exact position of the back sleeve insertion point is determined by measuring the back armhole of the side seam on the bodice to the sleeve insertion point; then another *1 cm* is added and its position marked on the sleeve piece.

Next the length of the head of the sleeve should be measured from the sleeve insertion point in the front to the one in the back with a tape measure and compared with the corresponding sections of the front and back panels. The sleeve should always be *approximately 10 per cent* wider between the front and back pieces and this should be respected when sewing in place, so that the sleeve hangs better.

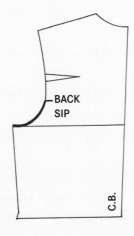

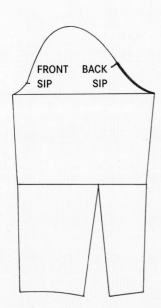

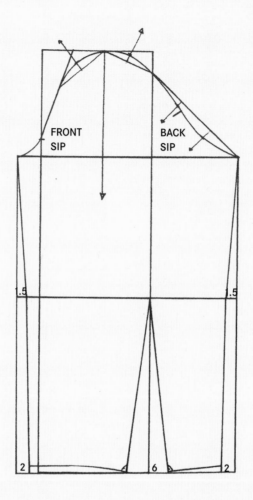

The side seams each have a reduction of *1.5 cm* on the elbow line and *2 cm* at the hem, to give the sleeve a nicer shape adapted to the contour of the arm and the right hem width.

Then the cuff width is measured, and the difference with the required measurement gives us the depth of the dart. This is taken in along line E from the elbow line and distributed evenly to the right and left.

Next the right side of the dart is angled to reach the side seam before returning to obtain a right-angled cuff. The side seam is then trimmed slightly. This amount is also taken in on the left side seam and angled towards the side of the dart.

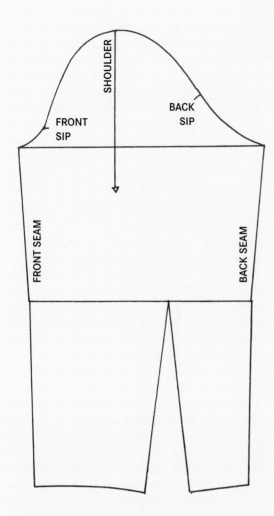

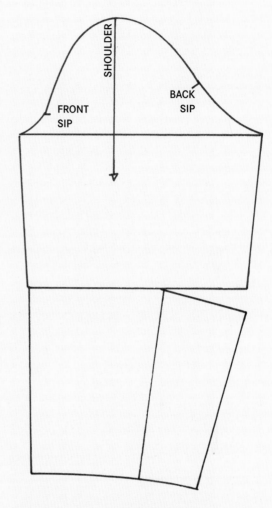

The drawing shows the finished sleeve with a dart in the cuff.

The dart can also be inserted and sewn on the elbow line in the back side seam. The advantage of this alternative is that the dart is much shorter and therefore less noticeable.

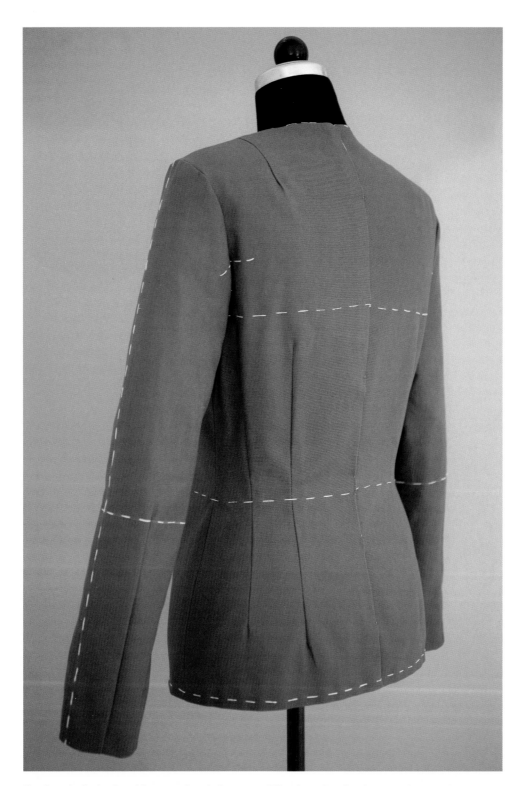

The darts in the back and front sections help the material fit the body properly. For optimum distribution these must often be adjusted individually to take account of the shoulder blades, the curvature of the spine, waist line and bust.

When inserting the sleeve, make sure the insertion markings are properly aligned. During the fitting stage, it is not uncommon to find that a sleeve needs to be moved slightly to the front or back, to hang straight on the body. The shoulder width can also be corrected at this stage. Further corrections for flat or high shoulders are explained on page 42.

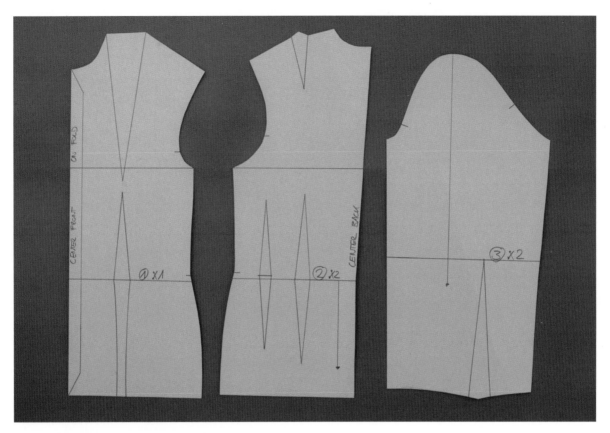

Basic pattern pieces for tight tops ready for cutting:

① Front panel, 1 on the fold

② Back panel, cut 2

③ Sleeve, cut 2

All pieces are cut out along the straight grain of the fabric. For the first fitting of the basic top –which is usually prepared using a sample fabric– a generous seam allowance should be used (approximately 2.5 – 3 cm on the side seams and 1.5 cm on the neckline and armholes). First the darts and then the side seams are tacked together with long stitches. The seams should not be oversewn at the beginning or the end, so that they can be ripped apart easily.

The seam on the back section is often left open and then pinned together right on the line once the garment has been tried on. The sleeves are inserted for the first fitting on the body, as described in detail in the chapter on fitting on page 40.

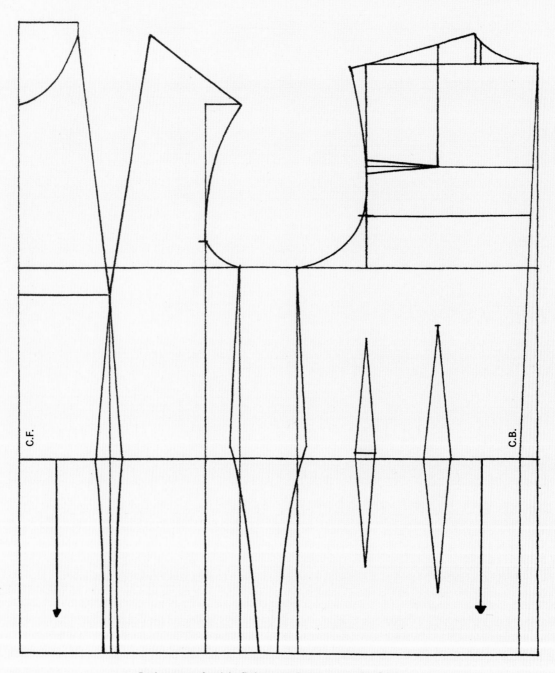

C.F.

C.B.

Basic pattern for tight-fitting tops drawn to a scale of 1:4

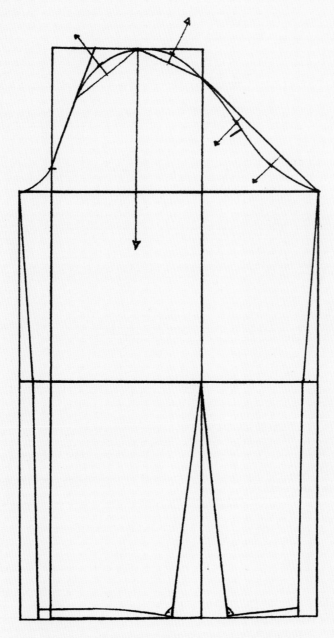

Basic pattern for classic sleeves with a dart drawn to a scale of 1:4

Tank top with wide pleats

This tank top combines a sporty look in the section with the straps with wide pleats in the bottom half. In the shoulder area the pattern should hug the body, unlike the part around the waist, which is much looser. Pleating is a very popular method for increasing width in a decorative way. The most common types of pleats are explained in the following pages, along with the concepts used in the description. After making up the pattern for the design, precise instructions are given for finishing the part with the straps.

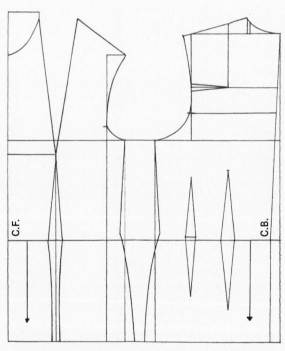

This top is generated from the basic pattern for tight tops. It reaches down to the hip line.

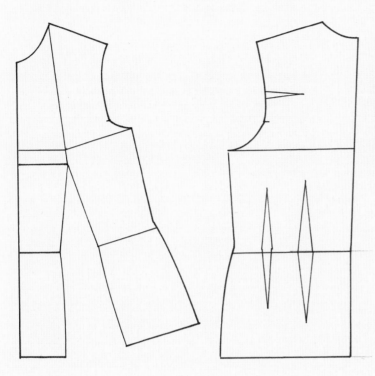

Since it is symmetric in design, half the pattern piece should be placed on the fold of the fabric. So that the construction lines can be traced without any interruption, the bust dart is placed on the front panel, and therefore rises from the waistline. The dart at the back, located in the armhole, should not be taken into account, since the construction lines do not extend as far as the dart. The waist darts are not needed in this design, which is loose on the body, and, thanks to the pleats, becomes even more generous around the waist.

The construction lines for the top are traced according to the design for this model. It is important that the front and back parts should meet perfectly on the shoulder and side seams. To do so, the neckline and armhole should be deepened (in this case, 3 cm on the shoulder line, and about 6 cm on the armhole) respectively. The straps have a width of 5 cm at the shoulder seams.

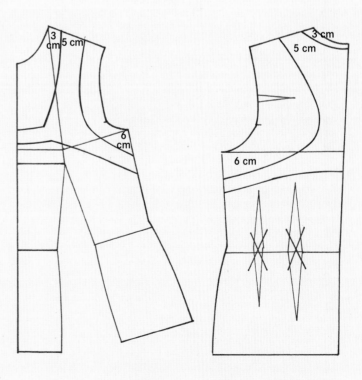

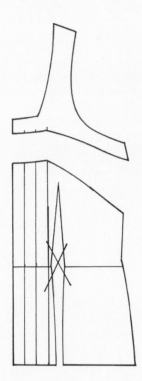
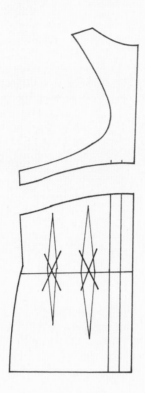

7 pleats should be inserted in the lower front piece and 5 pleats in the back. Since we are working with half of the pattern and the middle pleat should fall in the center front and back, 3 lines are drawn on the front and 2 on the back and their position is marked on the upper piece of the pattern. These markings make it considerably easier to stitch the pleats at regular intervals later on. The pleat distance is 2.5 cm.

The content of the pleat is 5 cm. Since the middle pleat is located on the fold line, the pattern piece needs only half the allowance for the content of the pleat, that is to say, a depth of 2.5 cm for each pleat on the center front and back line. The pattern is cut following the construction lines, and the depth of the pleat is added. The front part should have 3.5 times the content of the pleat, that is to say, about another 17.5 cm, with the back part having 2.5 times the content of the pleat, which amounts to another 12.5 cm. Before proceeding to cut, we recommend measuring the width of the pattern again just to make sure. The side seams are traced in a straight line, there being no fitted parts in the design.

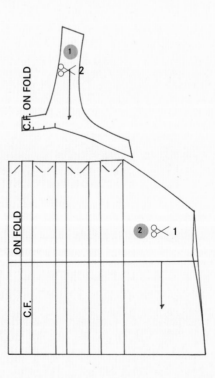

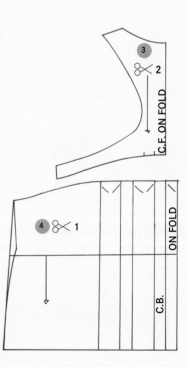

Useful information concerning pleats

Pleats are pieces of fabric that can be used to ease width. They may be sewn, and can be pressed or free falling. Each pleat has an inner and outer fold, and most of them are straight.

The line where a section of fabric is pleated is known as the "fold": the **outer fold** is located at the point where the fabric of the pleat is turned inwards; and the **inner fold** is the line where the pleat comes to an end. The following definitions are important:

The **distance of the pleat** (also known as the width of the pleat or pleat length) is the distance from one outer fold to the next in the case of closed pleats, that is to say, with the visible part of the pleat on the front side of the fabric.

The **depth of the pleat** is the distance from the inner fold to the outer fold and thus the part of the pleat that is visible on the wrong side of the fabric.

The **content of the pleat** consists of the double depth of the pleat, which is the total amount of fabric that remains on the inside.

In other words, each simple pleat uses the double depth of the pleat or the content of the pleat, and thus the *width of the pattern piece* that needs to be cut will always be greater than the *completed width* with the pleat inserted, expressed as *total amount of the content of the pleat x number of pleats*.

In keeping with the way they are inserted, pleats can be classified under the following categories:
There are **knife pleats**, which can run in either direction. These can be divided into *normal pleats*, in which the distance of the pleats is the same as the depth of the pleat. If the distance of the pleats is bigger than the depth of the pleat, it is known as a *wide pleat*. On the other hand, pleats in which the distance of the pleats is less than the depth of the pleat are called *narrow pleats*.

Box pleats have two pleats that face each other on the wrong side of the fabric.

Inverted pleats are worked in the same way as box pleats with the difference that the edges of each fold meet on the right side of the fabric.

WIDTH OF THE PATTERN   COMPLETED WIDTH

1. DEPTH
2. CONTENT
3. DISTANCE (WIDTH)

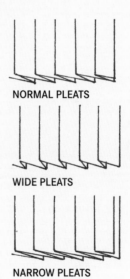

NORMAL PLEATS

WIDE PLEATS

NARROW PLEATS

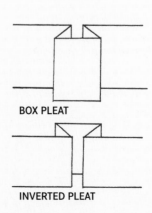

BOX PLEAT

INVERTED PLEAT

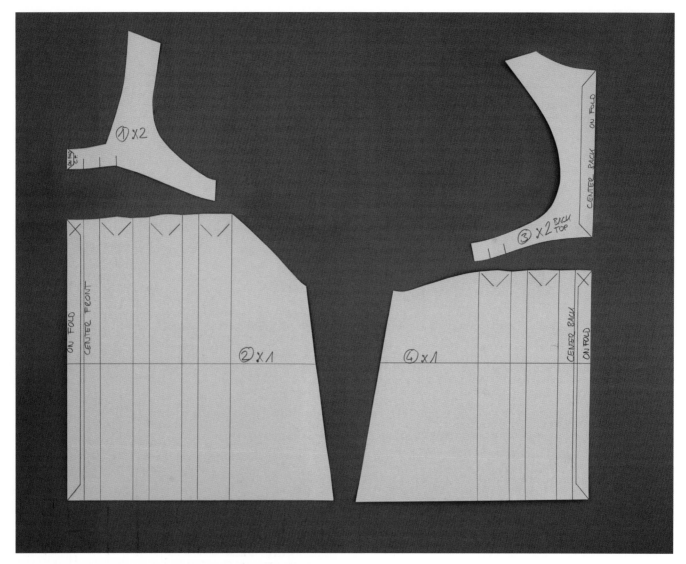

The prepared parts of the pattern should be cut out along the straight grain of the fabric:

1. Top front piece, 2x on the fold
2. Bottom front piece, 1x on the fold
3. Top back piece, 2x on the fold
4. Bottom back piece, 1x on the fold

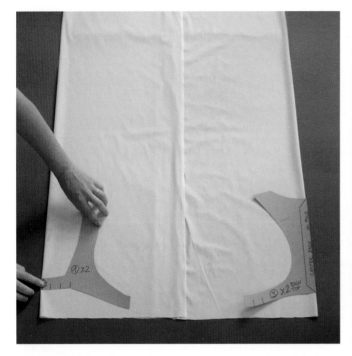

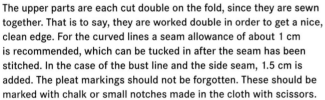

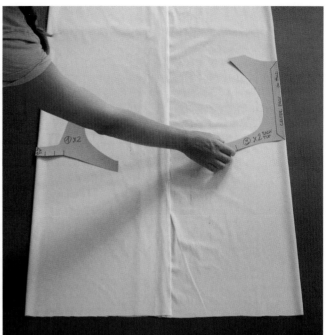

The upper parts are each cut double on the fold, since they are sewn together. That is to say, they are worked double in order to get a nice, clean edge. For the curved lines a seam allowance of about 1 cm is recommended, which can be tucked in after the seam has been stitched. In the case of the bust line and the side seam, 1.5 cm is added. The pleat markings should not be forgotten. These should be marked with chalk or small notches made in the cloth with scissors.

The bottom pieces are also cut out on the fold, but due to the extra width required, they are not placed right up alongside each other on the cloth. Since this fabric is not restricted to a single direction, either because of the weave or print, a pattern piece may be "turned around", that is, it can be laid upside down. Seam allowances of 1.5 cm on the bust line and side seams are enough, since there is no risk of this piece being too tight. Tiny notches are used to transfer the markings for the distance and depth of the pleats from the pattern piece to the fabric. For the hem an allowance of 0.5 cm is added.

First the upper front and back pieces are sewn and placed on top of each other. This means: the same pieces are pinned right sides together and sewn along the neckline and armhole with a seam allowance of 1 cm. The shoulder and bust seams are left open. A tiny notch is made in the seam allowances, particularly on the corner of the front neck piece, and the pieces are turned the right way out and pressed flat. Then the narrow seams along the shoulders are closed, using a trick that will be explained below.

The front strap piece is inserted into the back piece, and therefore the seam allowances on the back piece need to be tucked inside beforehand. Once turned inside out, the pieces should lie with their right sides together. The front strap is inside the back strap and can easily be reached across the open bust seam.

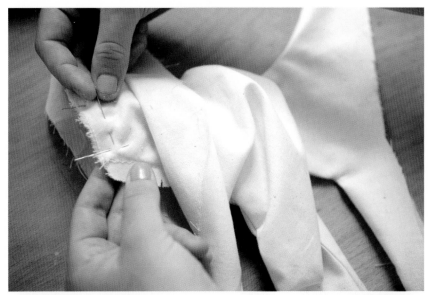

The seam along the shoulder line is pinned and tacked and the straps turned the right way round again. The shoulder seam is trimmed and neatened, with the seam allowance being tucked into the back piece. The right side seam is closed in such a way that the seam allowances remain inside.

The pleats are inserted in line with the small notches and tacked into place.

In the next step the side seams are closed, leaving the top half of the left one open, since the zipper will be inserted there. The hem in this case will be finished by trimming and subsequently sewing on a small binding, measuring 0.5 cm in this case. This will make the hem light enough to allow the fabric to hang nicely.

The pleated part is then tacked to the white top, in such a way that the pleats coincide with the markings. The pleats should fall vertically.

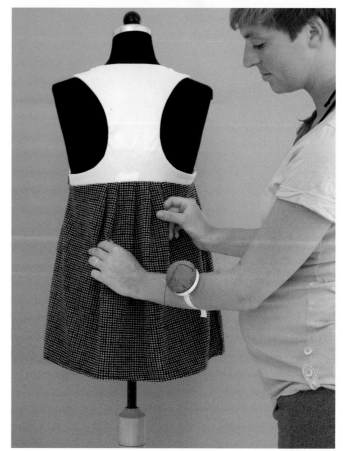

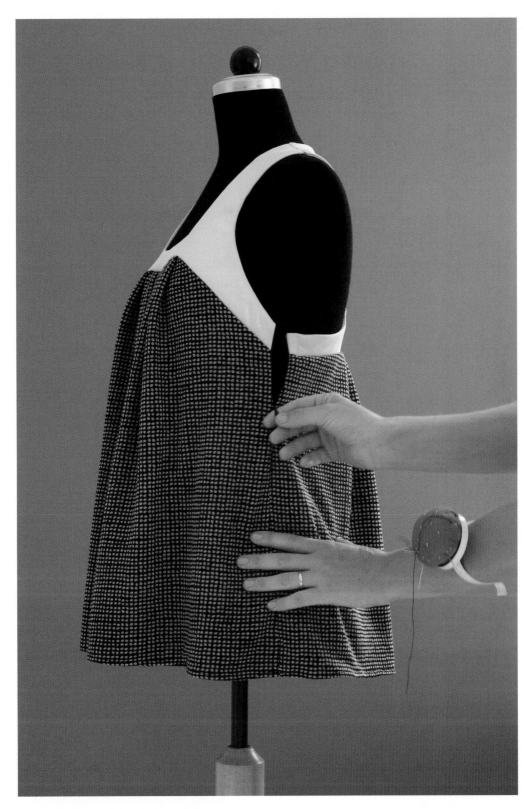

The invisible zipper is sewn into the left side seam. It begins about 20 cm from the bottom and extends as far as the armhole. The color of the zipper should blend in well with the multicolored pieces of the garment, to enhance its overall harmony.

Close-fitting dress with trimmed sleeves, waist yoke and visible zipper

The silhouette of this knee-length dress is not so different from the basic pattern. However, there are some striking effects that have been developed in this model due to some style lines, determined here directly on the mannequin, along with the use of several different fabrics. The sophisticated shoulder design with its bolero effect and the metal zipper on the center back are other interesting details. Step-by-step sewing instructions for this type of zipper are given at the end of the chapter.

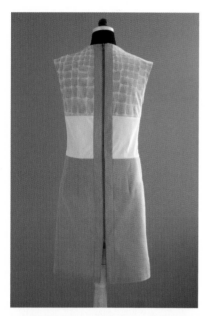

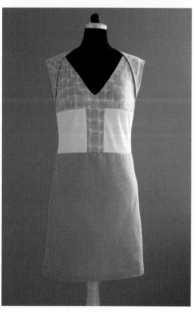

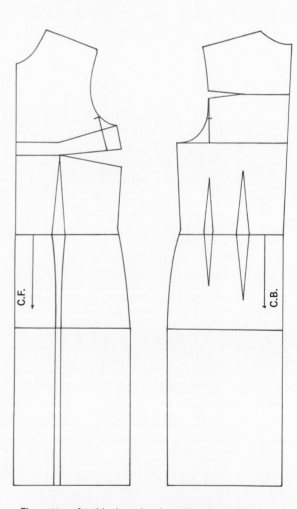

The pattern for this dress has been developed from the basic pattern. The bust dart in the front panel is located in the side seam, whereas in the back panel the dart is now in the armhole.

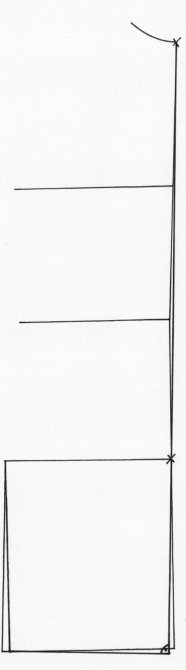

The center back is adapted to the fold line—which means it has a seam, but the zipper will be sewn in along a straight line, which will make it much simpler. Furthermore, the point at the base of the neck links up with the point on the hips in a straight line and then this line is continued down to the hem line. It is then taken towards the left to the nearest vertical seam. This will remove a small amount of fabric from the center back, which should be added to the neighboring seam.

The construction lines are now sketched in accordingly on the front and back panels. This features the divisions of the waist, the area of the bust, the skirt and the center back, along with the use of various different colored fabrics. A sort of bolero effect is achieved on the shoulders by overlapping the back panel on top of the front section. Since it demands a lot of imagination to draw the construction lines to reflect the sketches designed for this model, resorting to the following method can prove very helpful, namely, working directly on the mannequin.

Thus, the basic paper pattern is placed on the mannequin and the lines traced. In this way it will be possible to adapt the proportions directly to the contours of the body. The paper pattern is then laid out flat on the table again, and the lines are checked and adjusted. It is important to make sure that the lines joining up all the parts, particularly on the front and back panels, are perfectly aligned. The new construction lines are cut, and the various individual pattern pieces are separated.

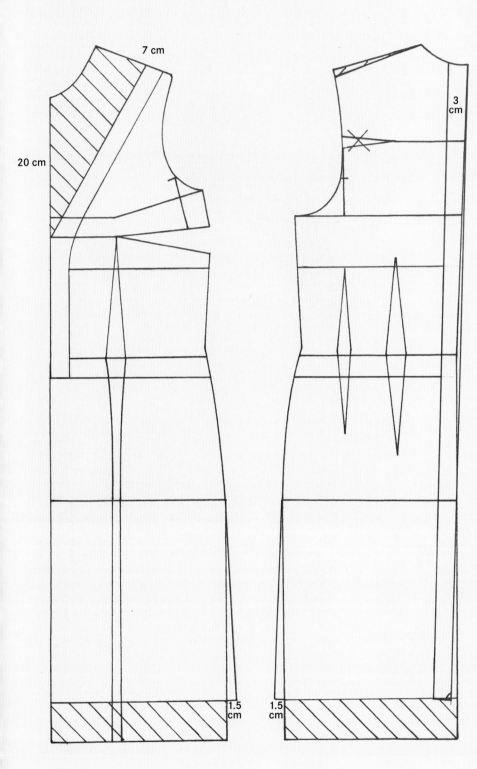

On the front panel the cutting depth is 20 cm below the neckline of the basic pattern and extends about 7 cm from the point where the shoulder meets the neckline, measured on the shoulder. On the back panel, the whole dart in the armhole is removed from the shoulder seam and can therefore be eliminated. Depending on the model, a separate strip, 3 cm wide, is distributed along the center back. This is visually appealing and makes it easier to sew the zipper.

The skirt is shortened on the front and back so that it measures 50 cm from the waist line. The side seams should be let out 1.5 cm respectively, to give a little more legroom in the skirt. The yoke around the waist is defined. Care must be taken to ensure that all divisions have right angles at their intersections.

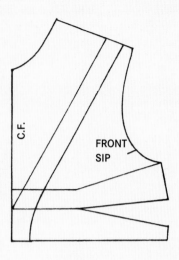

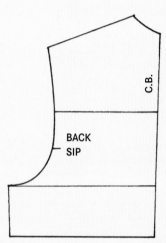

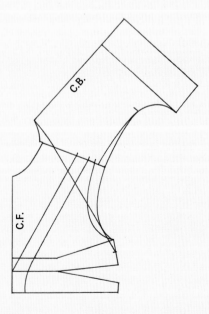

When working on the shoulders and sleeves it is advisable to join the front and back panels together on the shoulder seam. The whole armhole can thus be drawn at the same time on both parts, and the overlap of the back panel, which forms the small sleeves, can be placed in position. This overlap is added to the back panel, while the front remains unchanged. The point where the front panel (1 and 2) joins the invisible shoulder seam should be marked on the back panel so that it can be sewn later on. The place where the short sleeves enter the front section should also be marked.

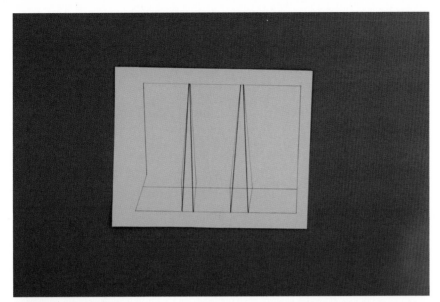

Darts at the waist will ensure a close fit, but with so many pieces, this would not be very pleasing to the eye. Using the model lines near the tips of the darts, these can be increased at pieces ③ and ⑥. In this way the same effect can be achieved, but without having any troublesome dart seams. To take in darts, the lines need to be drawn straight. The paper inside the dart is trimmed and the straight lines of the dart are put together. The pieces are then rounded off and the edges re-adjusted.

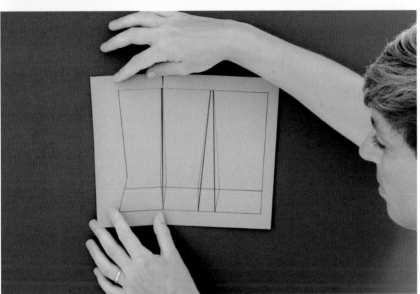

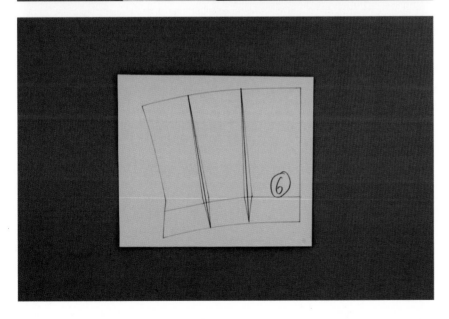

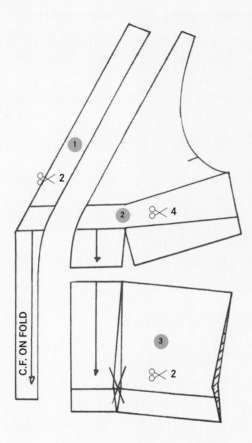

In pieces ③ and ⑥ the small remaining darts in the waist line should be taken into the side seam. Piece ① can now be traced. Once this has been done, the bust dart is inserted in the side seam on piece ②, and its width is taken down in the vertical dart in the waist line, so that it is slightly more open. This amount of fabric measuring about 1.5 cm can be stitched like a small dart, or as in this instance, as small tucks inserted under the bust and firmly stitched to piece ③.

In piece ④ the straight dart rises from the hip line, with the remaining width in the area above the hip line being taken up in the side seam. This dart thus also disappears for aesthetic reasons.

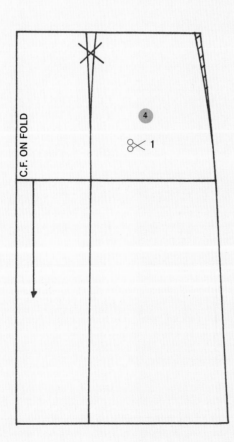

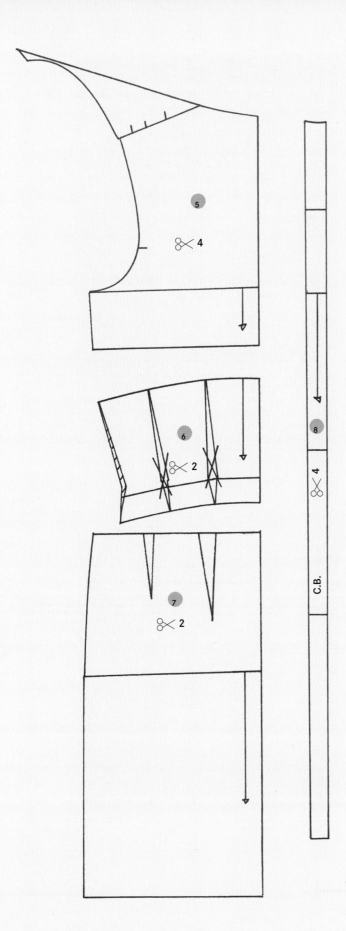

The back pieces ⑤ , ⑥ , ⑦ and ⑧ are separated from one another and thus ready for cutting.

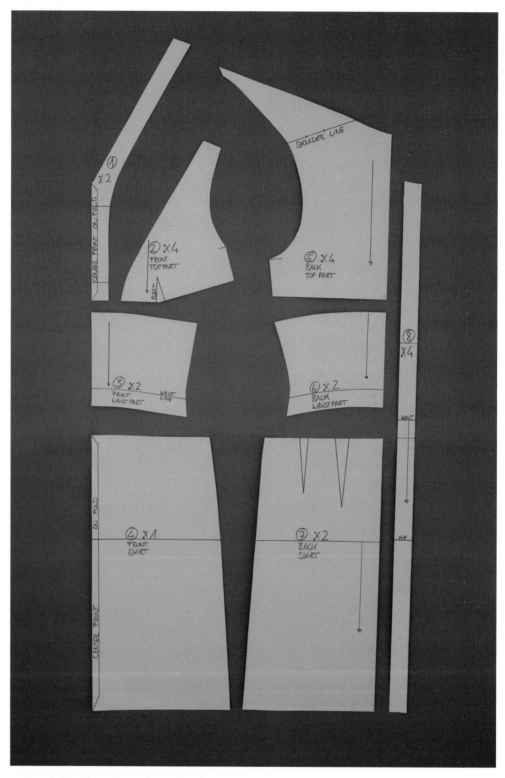

The prepared parts of the pattern should be cut out along the straight grain of the fabric:

1. Upper front panel, 2x on the fold
2. Bustier piece, cut 4
3. Front waist yoke, cut 2
4. Front skirt, 1x on the fold
5. Upper back piece, cut 4
6. Back waist yoke, cut 2
7. Back skirt piece, cut 2
8. Center back, cut 4

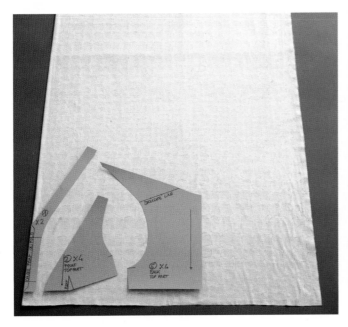

Piece 1 should be cut double on the fold; pieces 2 and 5 should be cut out four times each. The recommended seam allowance is 1.5 cm, which can be trimmed back where necessary, for example, on the curves, after stitching and pressing. 2 cm are added to the side seams.

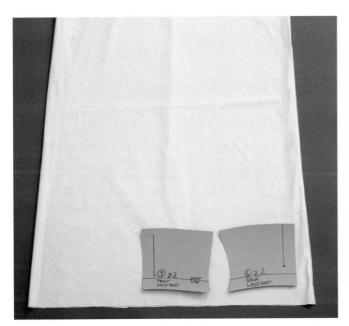

The white waist yoke parts 3 and 6 should be cut out twice. The side seams have a 2 cm seam allowance, and all other seams have an allowance of 1.5 cm.

The front skirt panel 4 is cut out once on the fold, skirt piece 7 is cut twice and piece 8 is cut out four times, since the same pattern pieces are used on either side of the zipper and also as the facing. The same applies here: A 2 cm seam allowance is added for the side seam and zipper, and 1.5 cm for the intersecting seams. The hem has an allowance of 4 cm.

The darts are sewn into the back panel of the skirt (piece ⑦). They are not so visually displeasing here and are important for a good fit over the bottom.

Darts are always sewn from the wide end and must finish in a fine point. Instead of oversewing, it is recommended that the last few inches are sewn with tiny stitches and the thread secured with a knot. This will make for a flatter transition. The fabric inside the dart is always turned in towards the center and ironed.

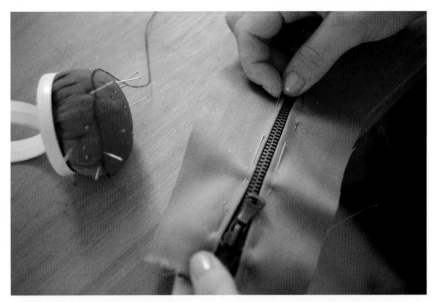

In this model a decorative metal zipper is incorporated in the center back. In our case the teeth remain visible, although depending on the design, the zipper can of course be concealed on one or both sides. This means that the fabric edge needs to be pressed and made to overlap the zipper, so that the metal teeth are covered. A special zipper foot on the sewing machine makes it easier to put the zipper in. Depending on the type of fabric used, strip 8 can be usefully stiffened with interfacing and the edges trimmed. It is essential to iron the edges straight, which should extend to the teeth of the zipper.

Start by pinning the tapes of the closed zipper on either side of the center back (piece 8). When pinning the zipper in place, make sure that the marks for the intersecting crosswise lines of the design are at the same level, in other words, that they coincide on both sides of the zipper. For inexperienced users, it is advisable to tack the zipper into place by hand to prevent it from slipping. Opening the zipper facilitates the sewing process. Both sides are sewn with the zipper visible. The row of stitches should leave enough space for the zipper to be pulled up and down easily, and should therefore not be too close.

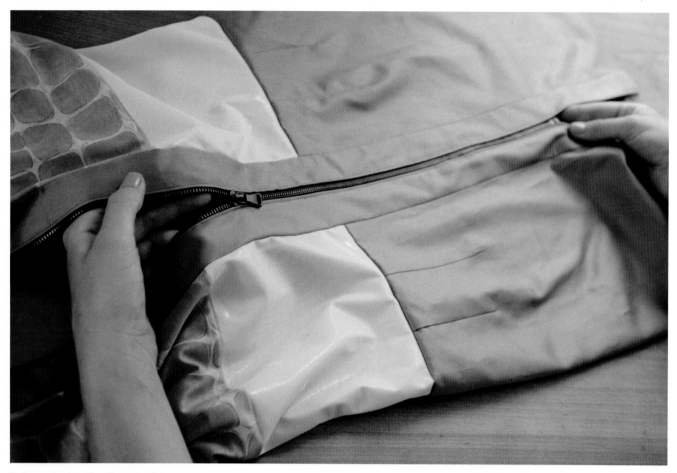

To leave the legs free to move, it is recommended that the zipper should not go all the way down to the hem line of the dress, but that a slit should be left open.

Yoke pieces ③ and ⑥ are joined together with top parts ② and ⑤. When sewing piece ③ to piece ②, the tip of the dart in piece ② is pulled into tucks. Then proceed to join it to piece ①. Next the skirt pieces ④ and ⑦ are sewn to the yoke. Two number ⑧ pieces are sewn to the center back.

Then the side seams are closed. The second set of pieces ①, ②, ⑤ and ⑧ are also joined together to form a second overlay, which serves to turn over the upper part of the dress. The same pieces are also placed together with the right sides of the fabric together and stitched to the neckline and armhole along the seam line. The lower intersecting hem lines are left open, so that the pieces can be turned over after the seam allowance has been trimmed. The seam allowances are then closed accordingly. This will give a neat finish in the opening and armhole area. The intersecting hem lines can be turned over and stitched to the inside seams, so that they do not come lose. The front (① and ②) is sewn into the shoulder line on the back panel, with the overlap on the back shoulder panel being held in place in the side seam.

Superimposed collars

A collar is always a good solution for finishing the neckline on a top and offers numerous possibilities for the style and final look of the garment. It can either blend in well with the rest of the garment or stand out as a striking detail. Depending on the way they are constructed, collars can be divided into several different types: superimposed collars are simply traced at an angle —as opposed to lapel collars, which are drawn out directly on the neckline of the front piece of the pattern. Typical superimposed collars include stand-up collars, and also shirt collars with a separate stand, which will be explained below.

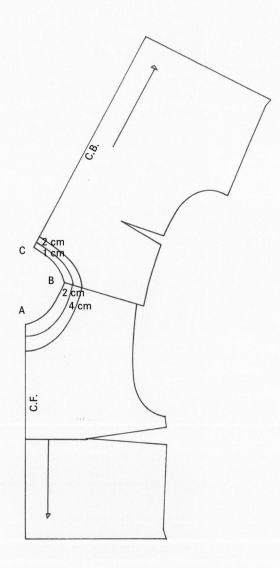

All collar designs can be drawn to fit a normal neckline or, if preferred, a larger one (when the collar needs to be further off the neck). It is important to alter the neckline on the garment at the front and back before beginning with the collar. Basically, the amount to be increased at the point where the shoulder meets the neckline (point B) should not drop more than half the depth at the center back (point C). Otherwise the collar will stick out behind or sag. The design on the center front (point A) can be altered at will.

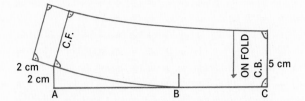

Superimposed collars are drawn separately, but should coincide with the measurements taken for the neckline. Begin by tracing the segment from A to C, which corresponds to the measurement taken for half the neckline, where A indicates the center front and C the center back. Point B is the shoulder point, i.e. the point where the collar comes to rest on the shoulder seam.

For the simple stand-up collar, begin at the line marking the base of the neck. The slight curvature is achieved by raising the highest point 2 cm on the center front (Point A). This will facilitate insertion in the round neckline. The center front should always be placed standing upwards and at right angles to the neckline. Where appropriate, the overlap should also be marked on the line of the center front, which in this case is 2 cm.

The overlap is the extra amount of fabric required on the center front for both of the upper parts and the collar, so that the garment can be closed with buttons, which are placed directly on the center front line.

The upper collar edge is formed by turning the collar upwards at point C, and decreasing the collar width, which in this case is 5 cm, parallel with the neckline round to the center front or the edge of the extra fabric added for the overlap.

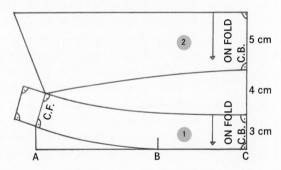

The stand for the shirt collar with a separate collar bridge (piece 1) is made in exactly the same way as the stand-up collar. This helps the shirt collar stand up. It is closed by means of a button and buttonhole. The neckline is curved round as far as point A, the top collar and facings are added and the collar insertion line is drawn parallel. In this example the collar bridge has a width of 3 cm. The widest collar piece (piece 2, which in this case is 5 cm and will be joined to the bridge by a seam, covering it in its upright position) will be made to hang properly by having a matching curve in the collar insertion line. This requires a specific distance—in this case, 4 cm—to be maintained from point C when designing the pattern and curving the insertion line downwards from there on. This should meet up again at the center front (point A) on the bridge. The upper collar edge in our example is straight, with the tip of the collar being shaped according to personal taste and in keeping with the design.

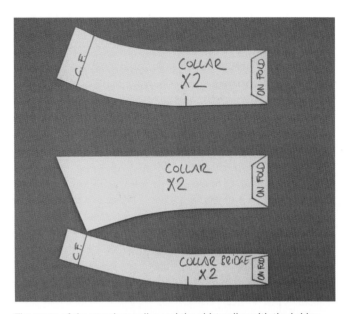

The parts of the stand-up collar and the shirt collar with the bridge or stand should be cut out together on the center back on the fold and on the straight grain of the fabric, with a seam allowance of 1 cm on the outer edge and 1.5 cm on the collar insertion line. For the collar fold line each piece is cut out twice on the fold. The parts of the stand-up collar should be stitched right sides together along their outer edge. They are then turned the right way out and pressed. The collar can then be stitched to the top along the insertion line.

For the classic shirt collar the pieces marked 2 are first stitched right sides together along their outer edge and turned over. That is to say, the right side is turned outwards, and then both are inserted between the pieces of the bridge. Thus piece 2, which has now been turned over, lies between the number 1 pieces, which lie with their right sides facing inwards. After stitching the curved insertion seam, the pieces of the collar bridge are folded and the collar is inserted straight inside, enabling the shirt collar to lie flat on the top. Thanks to the curved seam line, the collar is arranged perfectly.

Lapel collar

The lapel collar belongs to the category of collars that are drawn out directly on the front piece of the pattern. It is the classic collar for jackets and suits and comes in a number of variations with respect to line and depth. Thus, it can be developed into a shawl collar, which is a continuous collar cut in one from the outer edge of the garment. The beautiful continuous lapel collar is very challenging to make. Therefore, in the next few pages we shall not only explain how to design the pattern pieces, but also provide step-by-step instructions for putting them all together as well.

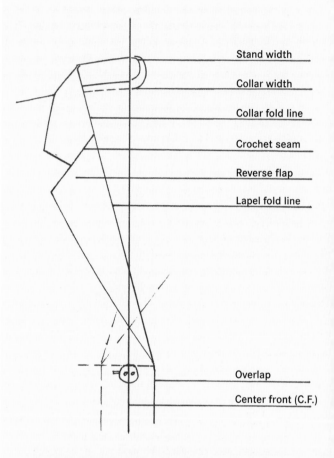

To design the lapel collar you need to make yourself familiar with these terms. You should then decide on how much overlap you want on the center front of the top and also how low you want the neckline by placing the top button in position in keeping with your design.

The lapel fold line, which goes over the collar fold line, marks the upper edge of the folded lapel. The width, shape and position of the reverse flap and tip of the collar depend on the design. The crochet seam is made in the place where the collar meets the reverse flap. As with the shirt collar, the stand, or bridge, helps the whole collar stand up properly. The stand and collar width must be determined by the design. However, the collar width in this instance should not exceed 7 cm, otherwise a different method would need to be used to construct it.

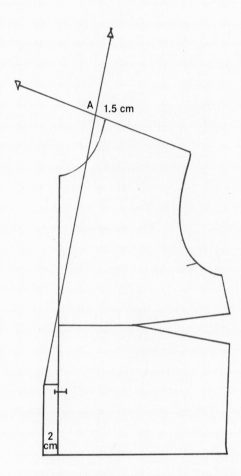

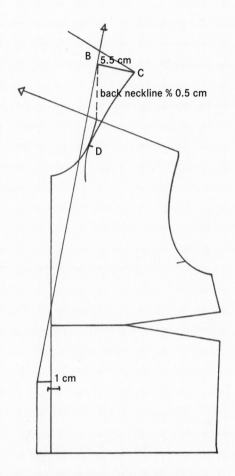

For constructing the lapel collar, first of all the bust dart is aligned with the waistline or side, so as to obtain a continuous shoulder line. Then the shoulder line is extended over the neckline, and the amount equaling the *width of the collar stand at the back % 0.5 cm* is removed from the point where the shoulder meets the neckline. This gives us point A. In our example the collar stand has a width of 2 cm. According to the formula mentioned above, this means that point A is 1.5 cm from the shoulder point.

The overlap is marked on the center front, which in our example amounts to 2 cm and the position of the top buttonhole is determined. The lapel fold line always begins 1 cm above and passes over the shoulder line through point A. It is on this line that the lapel will subsequently be turned over.

To obtain point B, a reference line is traced upwards measuring *back neckline formula % 0.5 cm*. This reference line goes from the convergence point of the shoulder and neckline to the fold line, so that the end point intersects the lapel fold line perfectly.

Point C is obtained by tracing a line perpendicular to the previous guide line from point B towards the right measuring the same length as the required width of the collar, which in this case is 5.5 cm.

From here there is a curved line running about 4 cm below the shoulder on the neckline (point D) and continuing about an inch or so beyond. Point D is used as the reference point to trace a diagonal line with the tailor's square running left from point C.

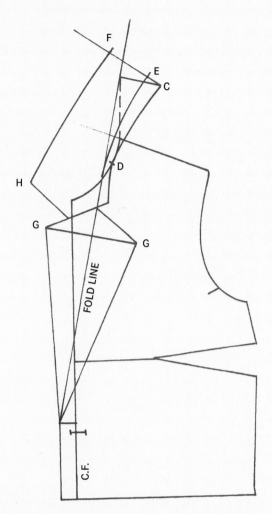

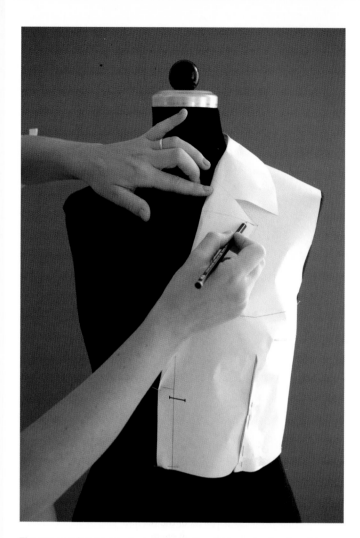

From point C onwards the width of the collar stand—which in this case amounts to 2 cm—should be marked off along this line, giving us point E. From this point we mark the width of the collar—which in this case is 5.5 cm—which will give us point F.

Point G is then marked for the outer tip of the lapel, the position of which will depend on the design. In this case point G is about 6 cm from the edge of the fold line. The illustration shows the reverse flap and point G in the unfolded position (on the left, as the outer edge of the pattern will eventually look) and what it will look like when folded (on the right). So as to better gauge the shape of the lapel, it is easier to draw the corner point of the lapel (G), firstly from the fold line towards the right and then draw the mirror image from the fold line towards the left. From point G a straight line is traced down to the overlap (in this case to a length of 24 cm) and the exit point for the lapel fold line, with another shorter line being projected towards the prolongation of the line running from C to D. The exact point is determined by the shape of the reverse flap, which will remain behind the fold line. This is the so-called crochet seam, the insertion seam of the collar. Point H marks the tip of the collar and is calculated at a rough glance in relation to point G.

Point H and point F are joined together by a more or less curved line (to suit the taste of the individual), which is the outer collar line. From point E the line of the collar stand or bridge meets the fold line, this being the fold line for the collar stand.

The reverse flap is drawn on the pattern of the center front and is then folded on the fold line. To achieve optimum distribution of the collar and lapel, often the simplest thing to do is to try the pattern directly up against the bust.

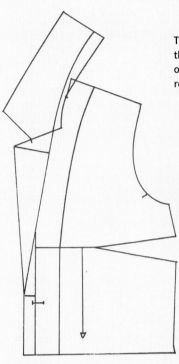

The lapel can be drawn "falling" on the chest, which means that the tip of the reverse flap appears to fall with respect to the tip of the collar.

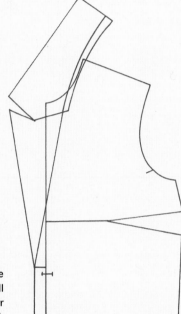

In peaked lapels the tip of the reverse flap rises from the crochet seam. In all types of lapel the corners of the collar can either be drawn as angular or curved.

In shawl collars the lapel is drawn as a continuous curve without any notches. It only differs from the lapel collar in its construction in the outer shape of the collar, which has no notches or crochet seam in the shawl collar. Instead of defining points G and H, a slightly curved continuous line is traced from the overlap to point F.

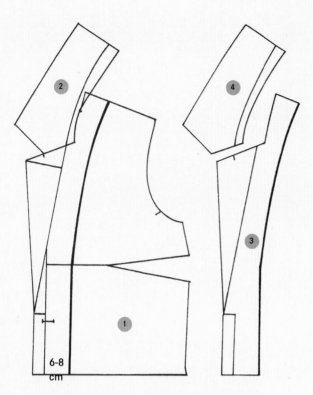

Since the lapel collar is folded over, i.e. with the wrong side of the fabric on the outside, it is essential to create a top collar (piece ④) and a front facing (piece ③), which should also be cut from the main fabric. These will be visible on the outside of the garment. To make this easier to distinguish, the top collar and front facing have been made from a shiny material in this example (see page 104). The top collar covers the collar, and the front facing covers the reverse flap. The facing is cut in keeping with the design, and is basically a copy of the front piece with a reverse flap. It does not extend the full width of the center piece but continues with an even width of 6 – 8 cm as far as the top buttonhole, before curving in towards the shoulder. The pattern for the lining should be placed on this line. That is to say, it should run from the side seam to the facing line and cover the remainder of the front piece.

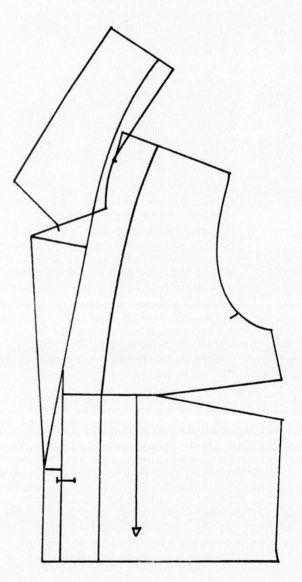

The lapel collar drawn to a scale of 1:4

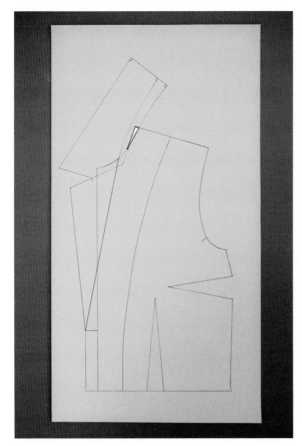

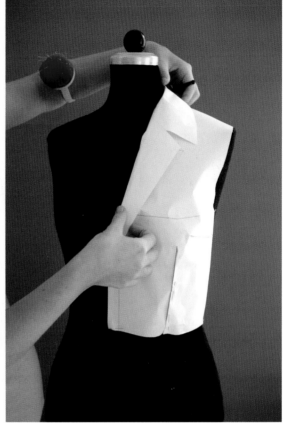

All the parts should be copied from the layout for the lapel collar. In other words, collar facing ②and top collar (④), front (①) and front facing (③). It is no easy matter to cut these pieces out, since the collar insertion line intersects the tip of the neckline. This means they share a piece of the paper which would be lost should the pieces become separated. Therefore, when copying the pieces for the pattern, all variations for the lapel should be taken into consideration at the corner (marked white in the photo), which should be cut on the collar and also on the front piece.

Both the proportions and shape of the collar and the lapel require a great deal of practice. We recommend always pinning the paper pattern on a mannequin so that the effect on the shoulder, neck and opening of the garment can be seen directly.

Depending on the thickness of the fabric, a width of about 0.2 – 0.5 cm should be added to the top collar and front facing for the collar fold line allowance, to enable them to cover the collar facing and lapel without pulling. In most cases, the collar facing should be cut on the bias, so that it hangs more pleasingly on the neck. It can either be cut on the fold or with a seam down the center back. Since a pattern cut on the bias often requires a greater amount of fabric, resulting in a lot of waste, in this case we can work with the variation incorporating one seam, as the collar facing will subsequently be covered by the top collar. The top collar is sometimes not cut on the bias because of the type of print, but placed on the fold of the straight grain, and therefore no seam is needed at the back.

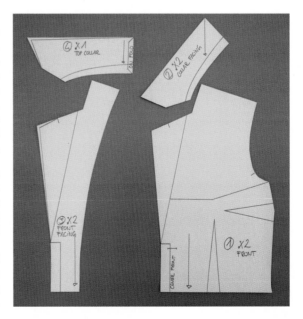

The pattern pieces for the front and facings:
① Front, cut 2
② Collar facing, cut 2 on the bias
③ Front facing, cut 2
④ Top collar, 1x on the fold

To overlap a front piece with the appropriate piece of collar facing (pieces ① and ②) mirror images of the front facings and top collar (③ and ④) are always required, since when they are turned over, the right side of the fabric should be on the outside.

Front, collar facing, front facing and top collar are cut out. For the outer edges and insertion seams there is a 1.5 cm seam allowance, which is trimmed or graded in layers before turning over. To make it easier to follow, we have used two different fabrics in our example (gray for the collar facing and front; silver for the top collar and front facing). Furthermore, we have also only worked on half the top. With a complete jacket, first the collar facings would be sewn to the center back and then inserted in the collar opening.

First of all, both crochet seams should be closed, i.e. the collar facing and front, and the top collar and collar facing should be placed right sides together and sewn up. Since they will subsequently be turned over together, these pieces should be mirror images.

The stitching here should be very accurate and run from corner to corner, that is to say, exactly where the pattern piece ends. The seam should not begin and finish at the seam allowance, as is usually the case, otherwise it will not be possible to sew the corner. The ends should be finished properly.

The corner of the facing is then snipped with a small pair of sharp scissors and trimmed to within about 2 mm from the seam.

The cut facing is taken to the
corner...

...and stitched.

The crochet seam and insertion seam for the collar are pressed open and checked to ensure the stitching has not caused any puckering.

Now the front and facing are turned over. They are therefore placed right sides together. The seam extends from the crochet insertion point down to the hem. So that both stitching ends of the crochet seam overlap perfectly, they should be pinned together exactly in the right place.

When turning over, the front and facing are pinned together along the front edge. The roll width of the facing allowed in the pattern should be maintained, and distributed evenly between the pins. The edges should be stitched together. The roll width should be stitched without any puckering.

In the next step the collars are turned over, with the pin placed crosswise in the crochet insertion point being extremely important. The seam of the top collar with facing and the collar seam should be stitched to within a gap of about 1 – 2 mm, and should never be sewn over the seam allowances of the crochet seam. Only by so doing will it be possible to achieve a nice corner when the collar is turned over. The roll width of the collar is maintained in the same way as the facing, so that, when turned over, the top collar will look nice on top of the collar facing.

The seam allowances and tips of the corners should be trimmed in keeping with the thickness and type of threads in the fabric or else folded over when turning the collar over.

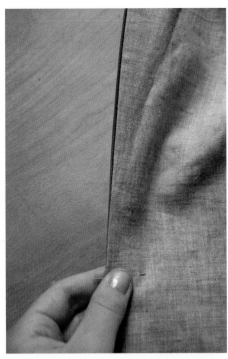

The seams should be turned over and pressed. When doing so special care should be taken. From the hem of the jacket to the top button of the front (gray fabric) should cover the facing, and should therefore be pressed with an overlap of about 2 mm. At the beginning of the lapel, that is to say, about 1 cm above the top button, the lapel falls on the fold line and covers the front. This is where the facing (silver-colored cloth) overlaps and is pressed into place.

The roll width added to the facing and the top collar should overlap the pressed edge very slightly, enabling the collar and lapel to be turned over without pulling on the front of the garment.

Glossary

A **bolero** is a type of small overjacket, in which the front pieces do not quite meet in the middle, but merely cover the shoulders.

Center back (C.B.): see Center front (C.F.)

The **center front (C.F.)** and **center back (C.B.)** mark the lines that pass lengthwise through the center of the body. When tracing symmetrical pieces, the half-pattern technique is used, which means working with a part that runs from the center front (on the left of the pattern) to the center back.

Cross markings are symbols marked on the edges of the pattern piece to indicate where lines begin and end. They also indicate the matching points for joining various pieces together. When the pieces are cut out, they are transferred to the fabric and shown as small notches or perforations.

Cut pieces is the term given to parts such as the lapel collar, for example, that are traced directly on the bodice and cut out as a single piece.

Cut two: see Fold.

A **dart** is a stitched fold of cloth that tapers to a point at one or both ends. It shapes the cloth to fit the contours of the body. In order to keep the tip of the dart as flat as possible, the seam should not be backstitched but secured with a knot.

The **dart intake** is the difference between the hip circumference and the waist circumference. It should be taken up in the darts and side seams, to shape the garment to the contours of the body. The distribution between various darts and the side seams is called dart intake calculation.

In the **description** of the patterns we use some symbols that, on the whole, are easy to understand at first glance.
- In a formula, the symbol % means "minus" and a hyphen means "up to".
- An arrow indicates the straight grain of the fabric.
- A curve with a dot in one corner means this corner is at a right angle.
- A cross over a dart means it is not applicable and should therefore be disregarded.

Easing means gathering the edge of a fabric so it can be sewn to a shorter length of fabric, without needing to make any creases or tucks in it. Depending on the effect required, the shorter side can also be stretched.

Edging refers to the act of finishing the raw edges of the cloth with bias binding or sewing over them with an overlock stitch.

A **facing** is a piece of fabric – normally cut from the same material as the rest of the garment – used to cover the open edges, such as the neckline or the waistline, to make them look more attractive. On the back of the collar it is used on the flap and is visible on the outside when the collar is turned over.
The lining is inserted through the edge of the facing.

The **fold or fold line** is the edge that is created when the fabric is folded in half. If a pattern is laid out on the fabric after being folded using the half-pattern technique, we will obtain a part in which both sides are completely identical. The fold line therefore appears to create a kind of "mirror image". A fold line can either be formed on the straight grain of the fabric (for example, by placing the selvages together) or else by folding the fabric on the bias.
By cutting pieces in pairs we would get two identical pieces like a mirror image but separated.

The **intake width** defines the amount of extra width that needs to be taken in.

The **interfacing** is often fusible material that can be ironed, and is placed on the wrong side to reinforce the main fabric, to line it, or prevent it from stretching or fraying. It is available in woven, non-woven or knitted fabrics.

The **lapel collar** is the classic collar on a jacket or suit. It consists of a reverse flap, a collar piece and a collar stand (or bridge).

Model lines are the lines on the basic pattern that serve to build up the design of the pattern. They show the placement of all the specific features on each design, such as seam lines, pockets, darts, etc.

Neatening the seam means securing the ends of the cloth either by serging or overcasting with a zigzag stitch, or else trimming it with the pinking shears. This will prevent the edge from fraying and be more esthetically pleasing.

The **overlap/placket** is the amount of fabric that should be added to the center front, for example, to accommodate a row of buttons on a closed jacket. The width will depend on the diameter of the buttons, and is normally between 1.5 and 3 cm. The button sits directly on the center front on the placket (in women's jackets on the left side of the front panel), and the buttonhole directly on the center front lap (in women's jackets on the right side of the front panel). When the buttons are done up, the lap comes to sit on top of the placket (i.e. the right side is over the left). If a zipper is used, it will not be necessary to have a lap and placket.

Perforation refers to the method used to transfer the pattern markings to various layers of cloth. This can be done with tailor's tacks – tacking loosely with thread through both layers of the cloth, or by means of a tracing wheel.

The **presser foot** (almost always made of metal) is the part of the sewing machine that holds the cloth in place as it is propelled forward by the feed dogs underneath and pierced over and over again by the needle. The "all-purpose presser foot" has two sides or shanks. The zipper foot only has one shank, thus making it possible to sew as close as possible to the teeth of the zipper. A special zipper foot is available for invisible zippers.

The **right side of the fabric** refers to the side of the fabric that will be visible when the garment is finished, whereas the wrong side is the inside. When cutting out, the wrong side of the fabric is on the outside, so that the markings can be made on the material.

The **roll width** is the extra width that is added, for example, for the top part of the collar and lapels, so that they can be turned over smoothly and pressed into place to conceal the seam.

The pattern pieces can be verified in the drawings that have been drawn to **scale** (in this case, 1:4). They can also be used for checking your own work. New designs are often converted into convenient small-scale drawings before they are completed in their original format in order to check the proportions, etc. Small-scale drawings are also worth keeping in the documentation.

A **seam allowance** is the excess fabric outside the seam line, which is neatened and normally pressed open on the inside of the garment. The seam allowance has a set width as required by the pattern.

The **selvages** are the edges enclosing both sides of a woven fabric.

The **serger** (also known as overlocking machine) is a machine that works with three or four cones of thread and a special sewing system that is used to neaten the edges of the cloth, while trimming the seam allowance at the same time. It can also be used with stretch fabrics and knits as well.

A **single-breasted jacket** is one that is closed by one row of buttons. With double-breasted garments, the overlap seam and the placket are normally more generous so that they can accommodate two parallel rows of buttonholes and buttons.

Sleeve insertion points (SIP) are the markings on the front and back of the bodice and on the sleeve cap that need to be matched up when sewing in the sleeve.

The **stand** (or bridge) is the piece of the collar that keeps it upright, and is covered by the collar itself when this is turned down. Shirt collars include a buttonhole and a button.

Stitch and turn refers to the technique of sewing two identical pieces right sides together, and then turning them inside out so that the seam allowance is encased inside.

Stitching means joining the pieces of the pattern together using a sewing machine.

The **straight grain**, or grain line, describes the direction of the warp threads in woven fabrics. The cross threads (or weft) run at a right angle to the straight grain. Pattern pieces are normally cut out on the "straight grain", i.e. in the direction of the warp threads or parallel to the selvage.

Superimposed pattern pieces such as superimposed collars, for example, are items that are made up as a separate pattern piece, which is cut to size, before being mounted and sewn on to the bodice.

Trimming is the term used to mean cutting away excess fabric from seam allowances. This makes the seam allowance flat enough to shape curves and corners. In concave curves it can be very useful to snip off small triangles to reduce the excess fabric from seam allowances.

Trimming the seam allowance (using the grade seam technique) is recommended on seams that join several layers of cloth together. Each seam allowance is cut away in layers, each with a different width, after the seam has been stitched together. This will enable the seam to lie flat and avoid looking bulky.

The pieces are cut on the **true bias** when they are at a 45-degree angle to the straight grain of the fabric.

Topstitching refers to stitching that can be seen on the right side of the fabric.

Wrong side of the fabric: see Right side of the fabric

Yokes are fitted pattern pieces, giving the body of the garment more shape. They are often cut double or stiffened with interfacing.

The **zipper pull** is the small part of the zipper that is pulled up and down to open and close the zipper. In invisible zippers it is the only part of the zipper that can be seen on the right side of the fabric.

Zipper tapes refer to the strips of cloth on either side of the plastic or metal teeth of a zipper. In most cases they are chosen in a color that matches the garment.